This Is MIDDLE SCHOOL!

Your Guide to Success

Keith Kyker

Third Stream Press

Tennessee, USA

ISBN-13: 978-1523831272
ISBN-10: 1523831278

Third Stream Press
P.O. Box 545
Sneedville, Tennessee 37869

www.thirdstreampress.com

This book is dedicated to all of
the great people I had the
privilege of working with at

Addie R. Lewis Middle School
in Valparaiso, Florida and

C.W. Ruckel Middle School
in Niceville, Florida.

TABLE OF CONTENTS

Author's Note

The typical American middle school has students in grades 6, 7, and 8. Of course, variations exist based on traditional arrangements and the needs of the school district. Some students begin middle school in 5th grade. Other students attend a K-8 or K-12 school.

When a student enters the middle-grade years, more emphasis is placed on student responsibility. Students navigate the school as individuals, rather than as a class. They attend a schedule of classes taught by several teachers in different classrooms. Middle school often provides the first opportunity to join clubs, play on school sports teams, and perform with the band and chorus.

Middle school represents a time of great change for students. Change requires adjustment. This book attempts to ease that period of adjustment and make the middle school years exciting and rewarding for students and their parents.

Introduction

This is Middle School!

What exactly does that mean to you? Maybe you're thinking about changing classes, and finally going from one place to another without a teacher escorting you. Maybe you're excited about the chance to play for a school sports team, or join the band or chorus.

And maybe you're just a little bit nervous. The middle school may be bigger than your elementary school. What happens if you get lost or if you can't get your locker open?

Before you get too worried, realize that thousands of students begin middle school every year. Your new teachers will be excited to meet you, and they understand that middle school is new to you. Is middle school different from elementary school? Yes it is! But those differences bring with them opportunities to learn, to grow, and have a lot of fun.

Freedom and Responsibility

In middle school, you have a lot of freedom, compared to your elementary years. You can choose the classes that make your schedule. You can try out for a sports team that plays against other schools. You can join the school band, perform in concerts, and march in parades. You can actually walk around school without being in a straight line with everybody else in your class.

And with freedom comes responsibility. When the bell rings and 1st period is over, you need to go to 2nd period by yourself. You may need to stop by your locker and get another book or folder. You need to complete your homework assignments and study for tests. You need to use your time wisely.

It is Different. You Will Make It.

When something is different, it takes some adjustment. But you will make it.

Maybe you used training wheels when you learned to ride a bicycle. If you leaned a little too far one way or the other, the training wheels made sure you didn't topple over. But one day it was time to remove the training wheels. It was a little scary at first, but you learned you could go faster and turn more quickly on two wheels.

Making the move to middle school is a lot like that. There will be adjustments. You will have to think about new things. But after a while it will be natural to you, just like riding a bike.

Don't be discouraged if you forget your locker combination. Don't give up if you can't find your 3rd period class. Don't cry if you take your history book to math class. Just keep trying, and you will make it.

The book you are holding now is about the differences between elementary school and middle school, and the adjustments that you will need to make. Reading about these things now will help you prepare for middle school.

It's time to take off the training wheels and have fun.

This is middle school!

Chapter 1

Your Middle School Classes

If you make a list of the differences between elementary school and middle school, changing classes is at the top. In elementary school, most of the day is spent in one classroom with one teacher. In middle school the bell rings every hour, and the students go to their next classes. Sure, elementary students go to PE, music, and computers. But, they go as a group and always return to "home base" – their teacher's classroom.

Some students are excited to begin changing classes, while others aren't looking forward to it at all. In the next few pages, we'll explore what it really means to change classes in middle school. We'll also look at how you are scheduled into those classes in the first place, and how you can do your best.

Usually a middle school has six periods each day. Some schools will start the day in homeroom. Attendance is taken and announcements are made over the intercom. These homerooms usually last about 10 minutes. Other schools will just tack an extra few minutes onto first period, and take care of the homeroom duties at that time. But typically, you will have six classes per day.

Those six classes will probably all be in different classrooms. Bells will ring at the end of each period, and all students will leave the room to go to their next classes. In elementary school, the entire class traveled as a group. Not so in middle school. Sure, you may have the same people in some of your classes. But, it is entirely possible that when the bell rings twenty students will go in twenty different directions.

Selecting Your Classes

A few months before your sixth grade year begins – probably sometime in March or April – you will register for middle school. Someone from the middle school will visit your elementary school. They may have a video program to share, or they may bring teachers and students to talk with you about the middle school. It is important to pay attention during these visits. A lot of information will be presented.

During this time, you will get an information sheet that describes the classes that you can take at the middle school. You will also get a registration sheet where you choose the classes that you want. Take these papers home and share them with your parents. Talk to them about the classes that you would like to take. You should return your registration forms a few days later. The school counselors will work on schedules all summer. They want you to have the classes that you select.

Your elementary school may also schedule a field trip to the middle school. Sometimes middle schools have an evening Open House in the springtime, so that parents and students can visit the middle school and meet the teachers. Try to attend these visits if at all possible. If the middle school doesn't have an Open House, you can certainly have your parents call the school and arrange a visit. Realize that the middle school setting is very different from the elementary school. Don't become fearful or anxious.

Remember, when you start middle school, everyone in the entire 6th grade will be new, too!

Your Classes

There are two types of classes in middle school: required classes and electives. Let's look at each type of class.

Required Classes

Required classes (also called core classes) are:
- language arts
- social studies
- science
- math.

Almost everyone takes all four of these classes every year they are in middle school. Each year you will study something different in each core class. For example, for social studies your middle school may teach world history in 6th grade, geography in 7th grade, and United States history in 8th grade.

Most middle schools offer basic, regular, and advanced courses. You will be placed in a class based on your success in school, your test scores, and your elementary teacher's recommendation. This way everyone can succeed while learning about the subject.

Don't be surprised if you have different levels in different subjects. Maybe you're a great writer, and you really love to read. You will probably be placed in advanced language arts. But at the same time, you really struggled in math this year, and you need some extra help. You might be placed in a basic or regular math class.

It's all about putting students where they need to be, in a class that is enjoyable without too much stress. If you're making all A's in a regular class and you're really bored, talk to your parents, your counselor, or the teacher. They may consider moving you to an advanced class. You can also have that talk if you're overwhelmed and stressed-out after a few weeks of advanced classes.

Elective Classes

There are four core classes, and six periods in the day. That means you will have the chance to take elective classes. Elective classes are classes that you choose. They are usually based on things you are interested in. Here are some elective classes that you may be able to take in middle school.

<u>Physical Education</u>   Physical education (PE) is one of the most popular electives in middle school. Some middle schools require PE classes and others make it optional. Most sixth graders take PE and they enjoy it very much. You might even get to choose from several PE electives, such as weightlifting, team sports, or aerobics. Students in middle school usually change clothes in the locker room at the beginning of PE, and change back to school clothes at the end of class.

<u>Art</u>   Your middle school will probably offer art electives. The type of art that you will create usually depends on the talents and interests of the teacher. Most middle school students have the opportunity to draw, paint and make 3D artwork.

<u>Music</u>   Most middle schools have active band and chorus programs. You can learn to play a musical instrument, read music, and polish your singing voice. Sixth graders are usually welcome to join the school band and chorus. Sometimes band and chorus members need to attend practice after school and participate in performances outside the regular school day. Make sure to learn about the after-school commitment before signing up for band or chorus.

<u>World Languages</u>   Some middle schools give students the chance to learn another language. Spanish and French are popular languages in middle school.   You will probably learn about holidays, customs, and food from other cultures, too.

<u>Technology</u>   If you like to learn about computers, you can take elective technology classes at your middle school. Most middle schools offer a class in basic computing. Topics like word processing, presentation software, Internet searching, and online safety will probably be covered in a 6th grade computer class.   Some middle schools offer advanced technology classes, including office applications, web design, and digital photography.

<u>Exploratory Wheel</u>   Middle schools want 6th graders to experience as many electives as they can. That's why the exploratory wheel class was made. An exploratory wheel class divides the school year (36 weeks) into three or four sections (9 or 12 weeks each.) In your exploratory wheel class, you might take art class for nine weeks, Spanish class for nine weeks, computer class for nine weeks, and chorus class for nine weeks. You get to "explore" all of those electives during the school year. Your experiences in wheel class help you select full-year electives for your 7th and 8th grade years.

<u>Remedial class</u>   If you have struggled in reading or math in elementary school, you may be placed in a remedial class so that you can improve your skills. For example, if you weren't very successful in 5th grade math, you may need to take a remedial math class as one of your elective classes in 6th grade. In that class, you will have the chance to improve your skills so that you won't have problems any more.

Don't think of a remedial class as a punishment or a penalty. It can really be a good experience. When you catch-up on skills that you need, you will feel so much better about school. Remedial classes are usually among the smallest classes in the school, so you'll be able to get help from the teacher. And the teachers who teach remedial classes enjoy helping students become successful. They won't judge you, and they are happy to help. In most cases, once you have improved your skills in the remedial class, you can join your friends in another elective class. The middle school wants you to be successful and ready for high school. If you are having problems in math or reading, it is best to take care of it now.

It's Your Choice!

Here's some important advice about selecting your elective classes: take the elective classes that YOU want to take. Don't worry about what your friends choose. They will still be your friends, even if you don't have the same elective classes. If all of your friends sign-up for computers, and you want to take art, then take art! People have different interests, and there's something for everyone in middle school. Just make sure you are choosing the classes that you want. Don't let your friends choose your schedule.

The Middle School Classroom

Several times every school day you will leave one classroom and walk into another. Your next class could be right next door, or on the other side of the school. Your next class could be in a science lab, a computer room, the chorus room, or the gym. You will also have traditional classrooms, with the teacher's desk at the front of the room and student desks arranged in rows.

Your teacher will probably have the same classroom all day. Maybe they have taught in that room for several years. Most middle school teachers consider their classrooms their "home away from home." Teachers decorate their rooms based on their tastes and interests. Some teachers feature posters and banners from their favorite sports teams in their classrooms. Others hang attractive and fun posters. You can probably find some family or vacation pictures in your teachers' rooms. Middle school teachers enjoy sharing their hobbies and interests with their students this way. You can learn a lot about your new teachers by looking at their classrooms.

Because your teachers consider their classrooms "home," it is important to treat the classroom with respect. You will have six classrooms during the day, but the teacher has only one. Don't run in, slam your books down, and start making a lot of noise. Teachers don't like that. Come in, sit down, and prepare to learn.

Seating Chart

When you enter the class for the first time, you will probably have an assigned seat. You might be asked to find your name on a note card on the desk, or find your seat by looking at a chart displayed on a projector. Some teachers have students sit wherever they want on the first day. They prepare the seating chart later in the week.

Be ready to sit where the teacher wants you to sit. The teacher gets to assign seats. If you're not sitting next to your friends, that's okay. You will be in the class less than an hour each day, and you can probably become friends with the people sitting near you. In most middle schools, teachers need to take roll every period. The seating chart is a quick way for your teachers to see who is absent. The standard "roll call" just takes too long.

Sometimes the seating chart will change as the year goes on. If the teacher has to ask you to talk less and work more, you can expect to have your seat changed. If your seating assignment keeps you from learning, talk to your teacher. For example, if the person sitting in front of you is very tall, and you're not very tall, ask for a seating change. The teacher wants everyone to be able to see and participate in class.

Your Classmates

You will see many different students during the school day. You may have a few of your best friends in some of your classes. You may even have the exact same schedule as someone else. But basically, each class is a new group and a new experience. Your 6th grade classmates may come from several different elementary schools. And of course, many students typically move from out-of-town every summer. The middle school is truly a melting pot!

Most students would like a class filled with their best friends. Understand that you can't get a schedule change just so that you can be in classes with all of your friends. That's just not reasonable to do for everyone in the school. There might be a good reason that your best friend's schedule is different from yours. Your friend might want to take band, or need to take remedial math class. A class you want or need may meet only once during the day, and your schedule will be built around that class. You will probably have time to visit with your best friends before school, between classes, at lunch, and after school.

A class filled with people you don't know gives you a great opportunity to make new friends. Making new friends comes naturally to some people, and is tougher for others. Getting along with people is something we all have to do our entire lives. When you go to high school, start college, and get your first job, you'll be around people you've never met. So make a few new friends. Do you have to become good friends with everyone? Of course not. But you will probably find that you have a few things in common with at least three or four students in every class.

Some of your classes will be larger, and others will be smaller. Your band, chorus, or PE class may have 30 or more students. A remedial math class may have 4 or 5 students. Most classes are somewhere in between. Whether your classes are large or small, and filled with friends or people you don't know, realize that everything will be okay and you will adjust. You certainly aren't the first 6th grader who needs to learn a new system. The teachers are there to help.

Class Time

The main reason you are taking a class is so that you can learn the subject. This might involve solving math problems, reading poetry, playing a musical instrument, or understanding an ancient culture. You may conduct science experiments, create an electronic presentation, or act-out a scene from history. All of these things will give you a greater understanding of the subject. Teachers spend a lot of time and effort making lessons that will help you learn. As a student, it is up to you to participate, keep up, and follow along.

Every class is different. In some classes you will take notes and copy information from a whiteboard or projector. You may read a few pages from your textbook and answer questions in a notebook. Your math teacher will ask you to work problems at your desk as she works on the board. In Spanish class you will repeat phrases aloud and learn common words. Your science teacher could create a demonstration in the front of the room, and ask you to write a paragraph about what you see. In history class you might role-play a character in a famous historic event. All of these experiences are different, but they are all designed to help you learn.

Your job: pay attention. Participate. Soak-up the information. Think about the class that you're in, not the conversation that you just had with your friend in the hallway. Complete the assignments. Cooperate with the teacher. Let the teacher lead the class. Do your best. Enjoy learning.

This is middle school.

Success in Class

When you're in class, give yourself every chance to succeed. If you need eyeglasses, wear them. Don't try to sneak texts on your cell phone. Don't ask for a bathroom break unless you really need it. Don't run into the room and sit in the back row. (Think about it – what are you telling the teacher if you do that?)

Do you have to be serious all the time? Of course not. Middle school is a lot of fun! Just understand that when class starts and learning begins, you need to be a student.

Getting Help

If you fall behind in class, ask the teacher for help. Be ready to tell your teacher what you don't understand. You may need to stay after school for tutoring, but you will find this time well spent. Your teachers want you to be successful and make good grades. Most teachers will absolutely love it if everyone makes an "A!"

The Importance of Reading

Learning how to be a good reader was a big part of elementary school. Now all of that hard work will pay off! Reading is a very important skill in middle school. You will read textbooks, handouts, and instructions. Directions for science experiments will probably be printed on a handout. Many math problems will be word problems. As you complete research projects, you will read from a reference book or a computer screen. Your teacher may give assignments using online tools. All of these activities involve the ability to read, and to understand what you read. Reading happens all the time in middle school.

If you're already a great reader – FANTASTIC! You have done the work in elementary school to prepare yourself for middle school. If you're not a good reader, you can improve. The best way to improve your reading skill is to

READ. Go to the library, and find books that interest you. You can read fiction books with settings that you like. You can also find books about exciting non-fiction topics.

Improving Your Reading

Reading is a skill – just like ballet, skateboarding, or basketball. Yes, some people are better at those things than others – but they all take practice if you want to improve. If you spend 30 minutes every day practicing your basketball free throws, by the end of the month you'll be a pretty good free throw shooter – or at least better than you were. The same is true with reading. You can improve with practice.

There are people at your elementary school and your middle school who can help you improve your reading. Your language arts (English) teacher is your biggest reading supporter. Your school library media specialist can help you find books on your reading level about topics that interest you. Most schools have after-school tutoring programs for students who want to improve their reading skills. There are also classes and services for students who experience learning disabilities in reading. If you have trouble focusing on the printed page, you may need eyeglasses. Many students get their first pair of glasses in middle school.

Good reading skills will help you in middle school, in high school, in college, and in life. Improving your reading skills will lead to success in middle school.

Learning Your Multiplication Tables

Math is taught and learned in order, as a sequence. Every year you learn new math skills based on lessons you have already learned.

Some students who enter middle school don't know their multiplication tables. This makes middle school math much harder than it should be. You will need to know your multiplication facts when you enter middle school. It is one of the basic skills of all math classes.

When you know your multiplication facts, someone can say "6 x 7" and the number 42 pops into your head. That's not a multiple-choice test or a button to click on the computer keyboard. It's not about your "best guess" or eliminating the wrong choices. It's about knowing that 8 x 7 = 56, all day, every day.

Learning your multiplication facts isn't really that hard. You probably know the words to your favorite songs. Learning your multiplication facts is much easier than that! The best way to learn your multiplication facts is the old-fashioned way – buy or make a set of flash cards. Get someone – your parent, your teacher, your friend, a school volunteer - to hold each flashcard for you. Make two stacks – the facts you know, and the facts you don't. Practice for about 10 minutes every day. Within a few days, the "know" stack will begin to grow, and the "don't know" stack will shrink. It takes patience and work, but you will learn your multiplication facts!

If you don't know your multiplication facts, you can expect the middle school to help you learn them quickly. Many middle schools give a quick multiplication test the first day of school. The test doesn't count for a grade. Instead it is used to find out who knows their multiplication facts. Students who don't know their multiplication facts go to a "math camp" during their elective classes. There they get the help they need. Why not brush-up on your multiplication facts before the first day of school? Once you learn them, you won't have to learn them again!

Handwriting and Keyboarding Skills

In middle school you will be turning in many written assignments. You may need to write a few words, a sentence, a paragraph, or an essay. You will need to communicate in writing. That writing may be handwriting, or computer keyboarding.

Many years ago, when your parents and grandparents were in elementary school, handwriting was a school subject just like math, reading, and science. Some schools still teach and grade handwriting, but most schools give very little time and attention to that skill. Many schools no longer teach handwriting at all.

Somebody Has to Read It

When your middle school teacher asks you to write a paragraph, he is going to be reading over 100 paragraphs – one from each of his students. Teachers really appreciate a paper that is easy to read. In elementary school, the teacher might accept a paper that is nearly impossible to read. In middle school, the teacher will likely hand the paper back to you and ask you to write it so he can read it!

The good news is that you can practice your handwriting at home with a pencil and paper. Make a list of your favorite songs, your best friends' names, or your favorite sports teams. Try to write as clearly – as legibly – as possible. Practice for about 10 minutes each day. (Don't write until your hand hurts!) After a few days, you will see a great improvement in your writing.

Computer keyboarding has taken the place of handwriting in many schools. Students may visit a computer lab at school or work on a computer at home. If your school provides computers, or if you have one to use at home, you should strive to improve your keyboarding skills. These skills include touch-typing (typing without looking) and improving your typing speed. There are many computer programs and web sites that can help you improve your keyboarding.

Homework

Most of your core classes (language arts, social studies, science, and math) will have homework at least once each week. Sometimes your elective classes will have homework, too. Here are some tips for managing your homework assignments.

Most teachers assign homework with 5 or 10 minutes left in the class period. You should write down the assignment and start your homework in class. If you have any questions about the assignment, you can ask while you're in the room with the teacher! This is better than looking at the assignment for the first time that evening at home, and being totally confused. Many students can finish some of the homework – or even all of the homework – during the class period.

Remember – teachers give homework to give you extra practice on what they taught in class. They are going to teach another lesson tomorrow, and they want to make sure you understand what you learned today. Do a good job on your homework. Most teachers give a grade for homework. Copying someone else's homework is cheating – just like copying someone else's test paper. Try your best, and do your own work. If you truly don't understand the questions, most teachers will give you an extra day.

Studying for a test is another type of homework. On Wednesday, your teacher may announce a chapter test on Friday. There may not be a homework assignment on Wednesday night or Thursday night. But the wise student understands the real homework assignment: study for the test!

So, what if you don't have a homework assignment or an upcoming test? Does that mean that you have "no homework?" Spend about 5 minutes going over the classwork of the day. Maybe your science teacher taught a lesson about the Earth's atmosphere, and you took two pages of notes. Spend about 5 minutes looking over those notes that night. Will you be online tonight? Do a quick search for "Earth's atmosphere" and see if you can find any interesting web pages, pictures, or animations. You will be surprised how much you remember from the lesson, and how much it will help in tomorrow's science class. It will also make studying for your tests much easier, because you've really been studying all week!

To review this section: manage your personal behavior. Be active in getting the help that you need. Practice your reading, multiplication, and handwriting skills. Be responsible with your homework habits. You can probably see how middle school will be different from elementary school. You have a lot of responsibility for managing your time, your conduct, and your education.

Grading

In middle school, the grade is the way that the teacher tells you and your parents how well you have mastered the course. It is a form of communication. When you earn an "A" in science class, the teacher is saying, "You have done an outstanding job in learning the science concepts I taught this grading period." A grade doesn't have anything to do with how much a teacher likes you.

You will earn a grade in every class that you take in middle school. Here are some thoughts about grading in middle school.

Getting Good Grades

Most students want to earn good grades in middle school. This is a good goal to set. Good grades are often rewarded in school, and you get to join clubs based on your grades. Making good grades shows your parents and teachers that you are a responsible student, worthy of extra privileges.

Students with poor grades are not allowed to play on school sports teams or join school activities until their grades improve. Students with poor grades have to attend tutoring sessions and take remedial classes. Middle schools often schedule parent conferences when a student's grades dip below a certain level. Some students get a weekly report card until their grades improve.

Different Grading Systems

You will have several teachers every day, and each teacher will have a different grading system. For example, in math class you may earn 50% of your grade on tests, 25% on homework, and 25% on classwork. Your art teacher may give a weekly grade based on your participation, and three project grades based on the art projects she assigns. Make sure that you know what's important to your teacher. That's usually what goes in the grade book!

Making the Grade

You will be proud of a report card with good grades, and you will probably enjoy school more, too. Decide now that you will strive to earn good grades in middle school.

Make sure you understand how your teachers grade. Their grading system works best for their subject. In Spanish class, your teacher will expect you to learn some words of the language. It makes sense that you would have a weekly vocabulary quiz. In band class, you may go the entire year with no written tests. Remember, the teachers have thought carefully about the best way to grade the class. Our examples – band and Spanish – are two different classes. You should expect that they would be graded differently. If you have any questions about how the teacher grades, ask during the first week of school.

Grades Based on Assignments for the Class

You will earn grades based on how well you do on the class assignments. Don't compare the grades you earn in your classes to the grades other students earn in other classes. If you are in advanced math class, your math assignments will be more difficult than the assignments in regular math class or basic math class. But don't expect higher grades just because the math is more advanced. Everyone is graded based on his or her assignments. The students in regular and basic math classes have the opportunity to earn an "A" just like you do in advanced math class. Comparing your grades to other students' grades is usually not a good thing. Instead, compare your grade with the goals that you, your parents, and your teachers have set.

Make Some Adjustments

In middle school, your grades won't be based on how clever you are or how well you've done in the past. Elementary school is easy for some students. They always make an "A" on everything, and never have to study very much. These students could see a big change when they get to middle school. For the first time in their lives, they have to study. They don't automatically understand the lesson. They have to ask the teacher for help. Make this adjustment if you need to. This is part of the normal school experience for most students.

Teachers Need to See Your Work

Really, the only way for the teacher to assign a grade is to see your work for the class. This is fair for you, the teacher, and your parents. Be prepared to show your teachers what you have learned. If you lose your homework, get out a fresh sheet of paper and start over. If you are absent, complete your make-up work. Your teacher needs something to put in the grade book, and that "something" is your work!

Accept the Grade You Deserve

Middle school teachers grade fairly. They want to give good grades. They celebrate "A's" with their students. But because they are fair, they give the grades that are deserved. If you get a bad grade, ask the teacher what you could have done to make the grade better. Learn from the experience. Apply the teacher's advice to the next assignment.

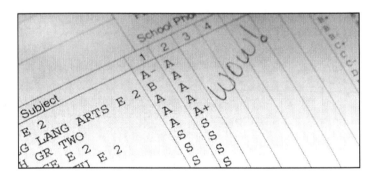

One Bad Grade

Maybe you've made only "A's" and "B's" in elementary school. You've never made a "C" on anything. Then, your first middle school math test is returned, and BAM – you get a "D+." What should you do? Run out of the room, screaming? File a protest with the principal? Call home?

Request a schedule change? No. Schedule a time to talk to the teacher – either after class or after school. Tell the teacher that you like to make good grades. (This will make the teacher smile.) Tell the teacher that you want to do better next time. (The teacher will still be smiling.) And ask the teacher what you can do to better prepare for the next test.

One bad test grade is not going to doom your report card grade. You can still earn an "A" on your report card, even if you started with a "D+" or worse. The important thing is to figure out what you did wrong, correct it, and do better next time. That might mean studying a few minutes more each night, going to a tutoring session, or taking better notes in class. You can do it! Just make the adjustments.

It's Up to You!

In elementary school, your teacher knew how you were doing in every subject. When you finished your math your teacher would tell you to work on the science assignment that you missed. In middle school your teachers will probably have no idea how you are doing in your other classes, or what work you need to make up for other teachers. It is up to you to use your time wisely.

Keep Track of Your Grades

In middle school you should always know what your grades are in all of your classes. Most schools have online (Internet) grades that will give you an up-to-the-minute progress report. If your school has this system, make sure you learn how to use it, and check your grades at least once a week.

If your middle school doesn't have online grade reporting, you can still keep up with your grades. It will just take a little bit more effort. Make a list of your assignments for each class. Keep all of the papers that your teacher returns. You will have a pretty good idea of your grade as the class progresses. With two or three weeks left in the grading period, ask your teachers about your grades and make sure there are no missing assignments in the grade book.

Extra Credit

If you find yourself just a few points away from the grade you really want, you may get to do extra credit work in your class. Some teachers offer several extra credit assignments, and some teachers never offer extra credit. The best "extra credit" is really to spend "extra time" on your assignments, and earn better grades throughout the class. But extra credit is an option in some classes. If you need a few points, ask your teacher.

Moving Between Classes

We'll end this chapter the same way each class ends. The bell rings – RING! – and it's time to move to your next class. We'll cover some of the finer points of changing classes in later chapters, but here are a few pointers.

Use your time wisely between classes. You may have a short walk to your next class, or you may need to walk across campus. It will take you a few days to learn the amount of time that you need. Remember, it is better to be a minute early than a minute late!

Will you be walking past your locker? If so, it might be convenient to trade-out your books and folders. If a trip to the locker takes you in the opposite direction, then schedule your locker trips so that you don't need to go at this time. This takes adjustment over the first few days of school.

You will probably also get to say "hi" to your friends between classes. "Hi" might be all the conversation you have time for! Don't plan for long conversations between classes. You will probably have time for those longer visits at lunch or after school.

The time between classes can be a good time to go to the restroom, especially if there is one on the way. Teachers don't like it when a student stands outside the door for two minutes before class, runs into the room when the tardy bell rings, and then asks to go to the bathroom. The time between classes is the student's time, and the class time belongs to the teacher. Don't expect the teaching and learning to stop if you're not there.

Important Points

We've covered a lot in this chapter. Let's review a few of the most important points.

- Select your classes carefully, with input from your parents and your elementary teachers. Select elective classes that interest you. Return your completed registration form on time.

- Respect each teacher's classroom, and understand that they get to arrange the classroom and create a seating chart.

- You might know only a few people in each class on the first day. Make new friends.

- Use your class time wisely, and understand that every class is different.

- Ask your teacher for extra help if you need it.

- Improve your reading skills, and memorize your multiplication facts. Make sure that your handwriting is legible, and improve your computer keyboarding, if possible.

- Begin your homework assignments during class, if possible. Remember to include "study for the test" in your homework list. If you don't have a homework assignment, read over the notes for the day and explore the topic online, if possible.

- Make getting good grades a goal for the year. Understand that each class will have the best grading system for that class, and those systems may be different. Learn how each teacher plans to grade.

- Your teachers assign grades based on the work that they see.

- If you get a bad grade, learn from the experience. Get extra help if you need it. You can improve your grades as the class continues.

- Know what grade you have in every class. Check your grades online if your school has an online grading system.

- Use the time between classes wisely. Learn how long it takes to travel from one class to the next. Take bathroom breaks and visit your locker between classes if you can.

Your Turn

How do you feel about changing classes in middle school?

What are you looking forward to? Is there anything you are concerned about?

What elective classes do you want to take in middle school?

If you were a middle school teacher, how would you decorate your classroom?

In class, would you rather work on group projects, or work by yourself?

If your teacher asked you to present an event from history, would you rather make a computer presentation, or act-out the scene in front of the class?

How would you describe your reading skill? Do you know your multiplication facts?

What are some things you could do to get good grades in middle school?

Chapter 2

Teachers, Administrators, and Other Adults

Another big change when you start middle school will be the number of adults you see and work with every day. Instead of one or two teachers, you will have at least six. You will probably see the principal, the assistant principal, and a guidance counselor. Another adult will coach the sport you play, or meet with the club you join. You may also talk with the school resource officer, deposit money with the cafeteria manager, get a bus pass from the secretary, and stop by the nurse's office for a band-aid. It takes a lot of adults to run a middle school!

Teachers

You will work with your teachers every day in school. In elementary school you probably had one or two teachers that you spent your day with. In middle school you will probably have five or six teachers. These teachers have different rules, habits, and teaching styles. The sooner you learn to adjust, the easier your school day will be.

Who Are Your Teachers?

Teachers go to college. In college, they decide if they want to teach elementary school (grades K-5) or secondary school (grades 6-12.) The people who want to teach elementary school take classes that allow them to teach any grade up to grade five. The people who want to teach middle school or high school choose one subject area (like science or social studies) and take most of their classes on that subject. So, your middle school teachers have taken many college classes on the subject they teach. Your math teacher is an expert in math. Your language arts teacher is an expert in reading and writing. Your band director is an expert musician and teacher.

Teachers Know Their Stuff!

Your middle school teachers will be really enthusiastic about the subjects that they teach. They take their subjects seriously. They enjoy reading about and talking about their subjects. They will have lots of interesting facts to share. Middle school is a great time to be a student!

Women...and Men

Most elementary teachers are women. That's just a fact. A typical elementary school may have a few male teachers, but not many. Maybe you've never had a male teacher. In middle school, you are likely to have men and women teachers. Get used to the idea.

Different Teaching Styles

Your teachers will make the rules and set the tone in their classrooms. Don't let that scare you. Teachers enjoy their jobs, and they are there to help you.

Different teachers have different teaching styles. Some teachers are very active in their classrooms, while others are more quiet and reserved. One math teacher may dance around the room, while the teacher next door quietly demonstrates math problems on the board. Your English teacher may encourage you to wear a costume and act-out scenes from your reading assignment. Your friend may study the same short story with a different teacher by joining a discussion group and writing thoughts in a notebook. One teacher may wear dressy business clothes and have a formal classroom. Another teacher could wear jeans and a sweatshirt and let you complete your assignment while sitting on the floor. Understand that all of these teaching styles are fine. All of the teachers are teaching the lessons. You will be learning in all of their classrooms.

Teachers and Technology

Teachers use technology differently. Some teachers are very comfortable using computers as teaching tools. They may present their lessons using PowerPoint presentations, videos, and computer simulations. You might be expected to create multimedia projects for your class. Other teachers are more traditional – books, wall-maps, and paper-and-pencil tests. This difference doesn't make one teacher better and another teacher worse. It's just part of their teaching style.

As a middle school student, it's up to you to adapt to these different settings. You will like some teachers and some classrooms and some subjects more than others. That's normal. After the first week of school you will probably be able to rank order your classes from "favorite" to "least favorite." But remember, that doesn't mean that your least-favorite class is "bad." Don't get into the habit of telling yourself that you have some "bad" classes. You're older now, and you prefer one type of classroom over another. Don't be surprised if your friend's favorite class is your least-favorite class.

Let's say that you're in the third week of school, and you have a class that you really don't like. You can't get comfortable in the class, and you're really not learning anything. The absolute worst thing would be for you to create a conflict with the teacher. Don't misbehave in class. You don't need enemies – you need help. Talk to your parents and guidance counselor. They may be able to help you understand why you're not enjoying the class. You might be able to get a schedule change. Expect the guidance counselor to speak with the teacher and ask why you're not enjoying the class. If the teacher says, "It's because he talks all the time and doesn't do his classwork," then it's really something you should correct. You would have the same problems in any class.

Getting Along With Your Teachers

Every teacher wants a good relationship with his or her students. However, sometimes conflicts occur. As a sixth grader, you will be stepping out of the elementary world and into the middle school world. Understanding what to expect will help your relationships with your teachers.

Make a Good First Impression

As the old saying goes, "you have just one chance to make a first impression." Your teachers will begin forming opinions about you as soon as they meet you. On the first day you should be on time and enter the classroom quietly. If your teacher has already assigned seats, then try to find your place in the classroom. Quietly listen to the teacher describe the class. Ask questions if there's something you don't understand. When the class is over, don't run out of the room.

Learning Your Name

Here's something important: your elementary teacher probably had 20 students all day, but your middle school teacher will have 100 or more students. Don't expect your middle school teachers to know your name after the first day, or even the first week of school. It takes a while for a teacher to learn 100 names. (You need to learn only a few teachers' names.) So, if your teacher doesn't know your name after the first week of school, don't be offended. Give them a chance! If your teacher knows your name after the first day of school, it's probably because they've had to correct your behavior. After your teachers see your work and listen to your participation in class, they will learn not only your name, but your personality as well.

Take Responsibility For Your Assignments

The best way to get along with your teachers: be a good student. Pay attention in class. Do your homework. Study for tests. Teachers appreciate good students. If you don't finish an assignment, take the responsibility yourself. Don't blame the teacher, your parents, or your coach.

Let's say you love gymnastics, and you go to the gym three nights a week. When you get home, you're too tired to finish your math homework. This is not a good excuse for your math teacher. You may be tempted to go to your math teacher and say, "I couldn't do my homework last night because I went to the gym." Although this is true, it's not going to make your math teacher very happy! You're basically saying, "Last night, gymnastics was more important than your class." Instead, try this: "I'm sorry, but I didn't do my math homework. I went to gymnastics last night, and I was too tired when I got home. I should have done my math before going to the gym. Can I please have an extra day?" Teachers will respect your honesty, and your ownership of the problem. You've obviously learned a valuable lesson, and you're not trying to get out of the assignment.

Taking responsibility also means knowing what work has been assigned, and when it needs to be turned in. Your teacher will announce each assignment to the class. Write it down! The assignment may also be written on the board or posted on the teacher's web page. If you forget the assignment or miss the due date, don't blame anyone else. Take responsibility for your assignments. If you made an honest mistake, your teacher will probably give you an extra day. Playing the blame game is not going to help.

Speaking With Your Teachers

It is important for you to talk with your teachers in a respectful, mature manner. Make good eye contact when talking with your teachers. Keep the interaction positive. Work on the ability to communicate your needs to a teacher. For example, we might expect an elementary student to say, "This is stupid! Why do we have to do this?" However, a middle schooler would be expected to say, "I don't  understand this question. Can you help me?" When you interact with your teachers, remember they are there to help you learn.

Remember to be respectful to your teachers. Be kind and courteous, and accept that they are in charge of the classroom. You will never win an argument with a teacher, so don't start one! If you have a question about a class policy, or you believe you are being treated unfairly, talk with the teacher one-on-one after class. If that doesn't help, talk with your parents, your counselor, or the principal about the situation.

Always Tell the Truth!

When talking with your teachers, always tell the truth. A lie may seem like a quick solution to a problem, but it doesn't work out in the end. Most teachers want to trust their students. Never give a teacher a reason not to trust you.

 Here's an example. Let's say Jack really wants to talk to his friend Sidney in the hallway between 2nd and 3rd period. So, he waits by her locker between classes, and they talk for just a minute. Unfortunately, when the

tardy bell rings, Jack finds himself still in the hallway! He is tardy. Wisely, he heads straight to Mr. Jones' class. Later in the class period, the teacher asks Jack why he was tardy. Instead of telling the truth and accepting the consequences (maybe a 10-minute detention) Jack decides to lie. "Oh, I was finishing a test for Ms. Smith's class."

Of course, the teacher responds, "Didn't she give you a pass?"

Our friend Jack has just traded a small problem for a big problem. Unfortunately, he takes another wrong turn. "No, she said to just go on to class."

Now Jack has lied to his teacher twice: the first time to cover the tardy, and the second time to cover the first lie! Jack's not realizing that Mr. Jones and Ms. Smith have hall duty together later in the day. Just as Mr. Jones suspected, Ms. Smith didn't keep Jack after class. In fact, she didn't even give a test today. It's not a good day to be Jack!

Something to remember: adults talk to each other. Teachers see each other in the halls, in the teacher's lounge, in the copy room, and many other places. It only takes a second for a teacher to confirm your story, and believe me, they certainly will. Don't put yourself in that position. Tell the truth to your teachers, and things will work out better in the long run.

Parties and Treats

Sometimes students are disappointed when they don't receive "treats" from their middle school teachers. Don't expect your middle school teacher to bring cupcakes for everyone or give everyone a prize or treat on Friday. The middle school teacher has too many students to make that possible. Think about it – your 5th grade teacher could probably buy everyone a cupcake for $10. Your middle school teacher has 100 students or more. Buying everyone a cupcake would cost at least $50. That's not going to happen. Middle school classrooms usually don't host birthday parties or holiday parties, either. Instead the party would be an event for a club or sports team. Don't get your feelings hurt. This is just one of the differences between elementary school and middle school.

School Administrators

Teachers teach the classes, but there are also people who make sure the school runs smoothly. They are the adults in charge at the school – the school administrators.

The Principal

There is one person who is in charge of the entire operation of the school, and that's the principal. Being a principal is a very important job, and carries a lot of responsibility. You may think of the principal as being the person who talks to misbehaving students and passes out certificates at awards day. But really, there's a lot more to the job.

The principal has to make sure the school operates every day. Here are some responsibilities that maybe you haven't thought about. The principal usually interviews and hires everyone who works at the school: the teachers, the custodians, the classroom assistants, the coaches, and the cafeteria workers. The principal also assigns work to these people (classes to teach, rooms to clean) and makes sure everyone is doing a good job. The principal pays all the bills, and makes sure the school is in good shape. The principal talks with parents and community members to make sure that everyone is satisfied with the school. Principals also have to be ready to deal with any emergency at the school. They make sure the students are safe by conducting fire and weather drills. Sometimes the principal is the first person there in the morning, and the last person to leave in the evening. It's a big job!

Your Principal is Ready for the Job!

Most principals have an extra college degree in school administration. Principals spend many years preparing for their jobs. Almost all principals worked as teachers and assistant principals before becoming principals.

Principals enjoy their jobs because they know they are helping boys and girls. The principal would probably rather be in the hallway talking to students instead of sitting behind a desk preparing a budget. If you go to a small middle school, you may have a chance to say "hi" to your principal every day. Students in larger schools may see the principal less frequently. When you see the principal in the hall walk up to him or her, give them a big smile, and say hello. They will appreciate that.

Assistant Principal

Medium-sized or large middle schools have one or two assistant principals. The assistant principal helps the principal with the job of running the school. It's up to the principal to decide what tasks to give the assistant principals. Your school may have an assistant principal who handles all of the behavior problems. Another assistant principal may be in charge of the school building: scheduling classrooms, making sure that repairs are done, supervising custodians, and maintaining the athletic fields.

Some assistant principals are interested in becoming principals some day, and others are perfectly happy working as assistant principals. Assistant principals usually have taken extra college classes in school administration, and they take their jobs seriously. Like the principal, almost all assistant principals started as classroom teachers.

Deans

Some larger middle schools have one or two deans that are part of the school administrative team. A dean works with the principal and assistant principal to make the school run smoothly. A dean may be a former teacher who is interested in becoming a principal or assistant principal one day. Some schools give teachers a chance to work as a dean one or two periods a day, just to see if they like that type of work. Other deans may already know that they want to move up the ladder. Maybe they just need more experience, or more time to complete their college classes. Remember, when you are talking with the dean you are talking to a member of the administrative team. Show them the same respect you would show the principal and assistant principal.

School Resource Officer

Your middle school may have a full-time school resource officer, or SRO. A school resource officer is a regular member of a local police department or sheriff's department who has been assigned to the school. School resource officers usually ask for this duty because they enjoy working with young people and they really want to have a positive influence in the community.

The school resource officer provides extra security for the school. He or she wants to make sure that everyone is safe at the school. School resource officers also help teachers in the classroom. The SRO will probably be a guest speaker on topics like Internet safety, the legal system, crime prevention, and social problems such as child abuse and drug/alcohol abuse. Some SROs coach sports teams or sponsor clubs for students interested in police work.

The school resource officer is also at your school to listen to questions and concerns that you have. It's nice to have daily access to a police officer if needed. Unfortunately, sometimes things happen on campus that need to be investigated by the SRO. These include vandalism (destruction of property), theft, and violence or bullying. Because the SRO is at school every day, he or she will be able to act quickly if there is a crime. If you become part of an investigation, it is very important to tell the SRO the truth. Lying to a police officer is a very serious crime.

Guidance Counselor

Most middle schools have at least one guidance counselor. You can talk to the guidance counselor if you are having problems at school or anywhere else (home, neighborhood, etc.) Your guidance counselor will listen and help you solve the problem. Guidance counselors have experience working through problems, and they usually know solutions that you probably haven't thought of yet. They can also put you in contact with people and agencies outside the school that can help you.

In some schools, the guidance counselor is the person you would see if you want to change your schedule. Counselors are also on the lookout for students whose grades are falling. The guidance counselor may arrange a conference with your parents and teachers if your grades go  from A-B to C-D. Some counselors are also responsible for school-wide testing.

School counselors take college classes to learn all about counseling. Some guidance counselors are former teachers, and others began counseling right after college. Remember that your counselor is interested in you and wants you to be successful in school. Schedule an appointment with the guidance counselor if you are having problems.

Library Media Specialist

 Your middle school will probably have a library media specialist (librarian) who is in charge of the school library. The librarian buys books and other resources, helps with research projects, and checks-out books to students. In middle school, you will probably not have a "library time" like you had in elementary school. Instead your teacher will schedule your class in the library when you need to check out a book for a book report, or you need to find information for a class project or report. The librarian may also be in charge of a

computer lab used for research. Students can usually visit the library before school, after school, or during lunch.

Most librarians were teachers before they began working in the library. They enjoy helping students find the information they need and books they would like to read.

Office Workers

Your middle school will have at least one secretary, and perhaps other office workers too. These people work for the school administration (principal, assistant principal, dean.) They answer the telephone, maintain the file systems, and keep track of the money. The office workers are in charge of checking-out students who have to leave during the day, signing-in students who arrive late, and issuing excuses when a student is absent.

As you can tell, the office workers have very important jobs in a middle school. As with all adults working in the school, it is very important to respect the office workers. Be kind to them.

School Nurse

There may be a full-time nurse or health aide who works at your school. The nurse operates a small clinic in the school where you can go if you're not feeling well. Nurses are trained to respond to medical emergencies at school. Some students go to the clinic to take medicine or receive breathing treatments throughout the day. The nurse will also call your parents if  you're sick and you need to go home. Some school nurses also speak to classes about health topics and health careers. A school nurse is a valuable person in your school.

Classroom Assistants and Tutors

Some middle schools hire classroom assistants and tutors. These adults help teachers teach, and help students learn. For example, an assistant in a reading classroom may help a group of students work on their reading skills. An assistant in math class could explain the solution to a math problem, or help a student who has been absent complete their missing assignments. Sometimes these assistants conduct tutoring sessions after school.

Cafeteria and Custodial Workers

Some of the most important people at the middle school are the cafeteria workers and the school custodians. If you don't believe that, imagine what would happen if your school didn't serve lunch one day, or if no one cleaned the floors or removed the garbage at night. You certainly wouldn't want to go to that school!

Custodians and cafeteria workers take pride in their work. They are often working in very difficult situations. Imagine if you had to cook for 500 people every day, or clean up after 500 students! As with all of the adults in the school, you should treat cafeteria workers and custodians with kindness and respect. Smile and say "thank you" when you see them.

Many adults work hard to keep a middle school running smoothly. They all have the same goal: to provide you with a good education. Treat the adults in the school with respect and you will find yourself surrounded by people who will help you have a fun, successful middle school experience.

Your Turn

What kind of teaching style do you prefer? Formal? Casual and relaxed? Somewhere in the middle?

What are some things you could do on the first day of school to make a good impression on your teachers?

Reread the story about Jack, who lied to his teacher about being tardy. What should Jack have done differently?

Would you like the job of middle school principal? Why or why not?

Think of three things you are glad that custodians do at your school.

Chapter 3

Your Friends

Friendship is an important part of middle school. In fact, if you asked middle school students why they come to school every day, many would say, "to see my friends." In this chapter we'll look at the relationships you'll have with your fellow middle school students.

Middle School Friendship Basics

If you've lived in the same city and attended the same elementary school since kindergarten, you probably have some friends you've known for many years. Sure, some students move away, and new students move to town. But if you look at your fifth grade class, many of those students were in your same grade level since kindergarten.

Middle school isn't that way. A typical middle school has students who attended several different elementary schools. So, your first class in middle school may have many boys and girls who you've never met. If you've never been the "new kid" before, this can be an awkward experience. However, all of these new faces will give you the opportunity to make some new friends.

"Friendly" and "Friends"

There's a difference between being "friendly" and being someone's friend. You can be friendly with almost everyone. Being friendly means saying "hello" and smiling. Being friendly also means helping someone pick up books they drop in the hall, or letting them borrow a pencil if they forget theirs. There's no long-term commitment with being friendly. There's no obligation to invite them to your birthday party or buy them an ice cream at lunch. You are being courteous and kind. Friendly.

Being friendly is very important in middle school. In class, you may be working in a group with students you don't know. Being friendly helps everyone cooperate and do well on the assignment. If you play sports, join a club, or play in the band, you'll probably be in contact with people you've never met. Be friendly with these people.

Being friendly lays the groundwork for future friendships. The person who you say "hi" to one day may eventually become a good friend for many years. Sometimes students say, "I don't have any friends." They probably aren't very friendly themselves. No one wants to be a friend to someone who is rude, grumpy, and discourteous.

Does that mean you have to talk to everyone, join every club, and buy the entire 6th grade a candy bar? Of course not! But when the opportunity arrives, smile, say "hello," and be friendly.

Are You Unfriendly?

Sometimes conflicts and arguments arise when people are unfriendly. Most people want to be accepted, and treated with kindness. If you act unfriendly to everyone, then people will think you are rude. If a classmate says, "Hey, we're going to the gym and shoot baskets after school. Want to come?" and you respond with a frown or a grunt, then you have probably offended someone who was just trying to be nice.

There is an enormous difference between being friendly with someone, and being their friend. If someone is your friend, you have an emotional attachment to that person. You care about them. You trust them. You want good things for them. You like to spend time with them. You would help them in a crisis. You would be very disappointed if you never got to see them again. Being friendly takes just a few seconds. Becoming a friend can take weeks, months, even years.

You probably have a few close friends already, and maybe you haven't thought about how you became friends with these people. Think about it now. You probably shared some experiences – playing, school, sports. You and your friend developed this friendship over time. You can certainly make new friends in middle school, but start small and be prepared to give it time. If you are friendly, you will find yourself becoming friends with people whose company you enjoy.

Different Relationships

"Friend" is one of those words that can mean different things. Thanks to Facebook, the word friend now means "anyone you know on Facebook." But not everyone we know is truly our "friend." It is important to understand the different relationships that you can have with your fellow middle schoolers.

Friendly to Everyone

Acquaintances

Friends

Close Friends

<u>Acquaintances</u>   You will have many acquaintances in middle school. An acquaintance is someone that you know reasonably well, and you might enjoy doing things with. Let's say you are in the band, or you play on a sports team. You are probably acquaintances with everyone in the band or on the team. You know them. You know a few things about them. Because of the activity, you spend

some time with them. But, when the activity is over you go separate ways. You probably don't call them on the phone, go to the movies with them, or invite them to your family cookout. You probably haven't spent too much time at their houses, or met their parents. They are people that you know and like, but that's about as far as it goes. Most middle school students have dozens of acquaintances.

Friends   As described earlier in this chapter, there will be some people in your life that will be very important to you. These are your friends. They are the people who you want to spend time with, and they want to spend time with you. You probably talk with them every day. You have several things in common with them. You would be disappointed if you didn't see them for a while.

Close friends   Within your group of friends, you will probably have a small group of close friends. This type of friendship often takes years to develop. These are the people you tell your innermost thoughts. They know your plans, your dreams, your triumphs, and your problems. They are the people you call when you really need to talk to someone. You feel comfortable being around them for long periods of time. If your mom says, "We're going to Disneyland and you can bring one of your friends," this is who you would take. If you have two or three close friends in middle school, you are very fortunate indeed.

Why do we spend so many paragraphs talking about friendship? Because it's complicated, and sometimes very confusing. That confusion can lead to hurt feelings.

Unfortunately, some people – young and old – want to skip the acquaintance step and become close friends with people that they just met. Most people aren't comfortable sharing their innermost thoughts and dreams with someone who was a stranger just a few days ago. That makes sense. True friendship is based on trust, and trust takes time to develop. Take the time to get to know someone before becoming their close friend.

Beware of someone who wants to get too close too soon; it shows that they don't have a healthy understanding of what friendship is all about. Making new friends can be especially tough if you're the "new kid" in school, and your close friends are hundreds of miles away. But a little patience now can save you lots of trouble in the future.

Can You Be Everyone's Friend?

You can be friendly to almost everyone, but you can't be friends with everyone. You shouldn't try. It would be exhausting. It's not healthy to become emotionally involved with too many people.

Making New Friends

Unless you have just moved to town and know absolutely no one, you will probably enter middle school with a good group of friends from elementary school. You might decide to keep that group of friends, and close off the possibility of making new friends. That would be a mistake. There are great people at every elementary school. You don't have to drop your old friends when you make new friends. Just keep your eyes open for people you have things in common with. It's hard to believe now, but you may meet your lifelong best friend in middle school, high school, or even later. Don't have the attitude of "us four and no more" in middle school.

There's an old saying that goes, "Make new friends, but keep the old. One is silver and the other gold." In other words, both old friends and new friends are valuable. Be open to new friendships, and keep your elementary friends, too.

Getting Comfortable

You should be comfortable around your friends. You shouldn't have to dress a certain way, listen to a certain type of music, or have a favorite sports team just to be somebody's friend. Real friends accept each other, and enjoy their differences.

If a person wants you to change your personality to fit their ideas, then they really don't want a friend. They want to be a king or queen, and they want you to be their loyal subject! Friendship isn't a boss/employee relationship. If you have to try too hard, then it's probably not the right group for you.

Loyalty and Manipulation

When you make new friends, make sure to understand what it means to be loyal to that friend. Certainly, you want to support your friend. You shouldn't say hurtful things about your friend to other people. If your friend shares something with you in confidence, don't repeat it to anyone else. Of course, if your friend talks about hurting himself or herself or someone else, immediately tell a trusted adult (parent, teacher, counselor.) Your loyalty to your friend does not include destructive or harmful behavior.

Also, be aware of friends who expect you to behave a certain way because of your friendship. This is manipulation, and it isn't healthy. Here's an example: let's say your friend wants to skip school one day. Your friend says, "All of my friends are skipping school. If you don't skip, then you're not my friend." That person is trying to get you to do something you don't want to do, and holding your friendship hostage. You can simply respond, "No, I don't believe I will skip school today." Your friend may respect your decision, or they may never speak to you again. Either way, you'll know if that person is really your friend. Friends don't try to manipulate each other. A friend will want you to be yourself, and make your own healthy decisions.

Your Reputation

Be aware that teachers, parents, and other students will make assumptions about you based on your choice of friends. This may not be 100% true, but it is expected. If someone doesn't know you, they will look to your group of friends. For example, if your friends get in trouble a lot, then someone who doesn't know you will probably think that you get in trouble, too. On the other hand, if your friends are honest and trustworthy, someone who doesn't know you will think that you have the same values. Is this fair? Maybe – maybe not. But it happens. Be careful in choosing your friends. Reputations are earned quickly, but tough to change.

A Final Note

No friendship is perfect. Friends argue, disagree, and make different choices. A friendship is not a lifelong pact. You may believe that someone is your friend, only to have them prove otherwise. Always make the healthy choice when it comes to friendship. If a friendship feels uncomfortable, talk it over with a parent or another trusted adult.

Changing Friendships

The move from elementary school to middle school is a time of great change. People change during this time, too. You will grow physically and emotionally in middle school. You will probably have the opportunity to develop your interests (like art and music) into skills (painting and playing a musical instrument.) Friendships change in middle school too.

Changes in Popularity

Sometimes students who are very popular in elementary school are not as popular in middle school. Elementary students who are taller, more mature, or more athletic are often the most popular. However, when compared to older middle school students, they will probably lose that status. The best elementary school baseball player may not make the middle school team. The most popular students likely won't be as popular as those two or three years older. The most mature sixth grader may look very young compared to the glamorous eighth grader.

So, if you're the king or queen of elementary school, what can you do about it? Remember that there's more to your personality than your ability to shoot a basketball. You're more than the clothes you wear. Don't tie your personal self-esteem to your popularity. Be realistic in what you expect. Even if you were the best speller, the best mathematician, or the best quarterback in elementary school, you may not be when you get to middle school. Be yourself. Be patient. When you get older, it will be your turn.

Don't Give Up!

You have probably heard the story of The Ugly Duckling. That duckling looked different from the other ducklings. His friends made fun of him. But when he grew he became a beautiful swan! He was never meant to be a duck. You will have your chance for success. Keep trying, and stay involved. Your body will eventually catch up to your dreams. Don't tell yourself you'll never succeed. Keep a positive attitude.

Changes in Appearance

Look at the adults in your life. They are all just about the same size. Sure, some are taller and some are not as tall. But almost all adults fit in the average size range. Why mention this? Because many students grow and develop in middle school. You know that little 5th grade girl with pigtails? Don't be surprised if all of a sudden she's spiking a volleyball on the school team. And that not-so-athletic 5th grade boy may grow six inches in a year and star as the goalkeeper for the soccer team.

Everyone grows … eventually. Some just grow earlier than others. Those who experience growth spurts while still in elementary school tend to be more popular and more successful in athletics. But everyone will catch up.

Changes in Friendships

Sometimes elementary school friendships change during the middle school years. Friends who were inseparable in fifth grade may drift apart in sixth grade. This is natural and normal, especially with all of the different activities available in middle school.

Here's an example: let's say you and your best friend have always played on youth soccer teams. You're an all-star soccer player, and your friend has been pretty good too. But your friend enjoys music, and is really looking forward to being in the band. When middle school begins, you make the school soccer team as a sixth grader! Your friend has joined the band, and is becoming a great trumpet player. You find yourself eating lunch with the soccer team, while your friend enjoys the company of other band members. You go different directions after school – the band room and the soccer field. You find yourself talking to your old friend less and less.

That sounds sad, but it doesn't have to be. Your interests have changed, and so have your friend's. Instead of letting the friendship end, make a special effort to involve your friend in an activity. Invite them to a movie, or get together to go shopping or play a video game. Attend their band concert, and tell them how good the band sounds. You will probably find your friend cheering for you at the soccer game.

The absolute worst thing would be to get mad and assume your friend hates you. They don't hate you. You have both developed other interests. Your friendship can survive. It will just be a little different.

Most adults can tell you about a friend they might see only once or twice a year. But when they get together, it's just like old times. That's when you know you have a real friend. It is important to be yourself, and let your personality shine through.

Before we leave this topic, we need to mention friendships that you have to leave because the other person is engaged in destructive behavior. Sometimes a friend will make many poor decisions involving things like school behavior, relationships, drugs, and alcohol. You can talk to a parent or trusted adult about these issues. But sometimes you have to separate yourself from this person. Your friend needs professional guidance, and as a middle schooler you're really not in a position to help. You can support and encourage them, but you don't want to get tied-up in destructive behavior yourself. This doesn't happen very often, but if it does your friendship may need to be put on hold until your friend corrects his or her behaviors.

Boyfriend and Girlfriend Relationships

Middle school is a time when many boys and girls become interested in the opposite sex. This is normal and natural. The way you express this interest and manage your relationships is very important.

Many middle schoolers enjoy going places in groups that include boys and girls. Maybe you can organize a trip to the movies, a skating party, or a meal at a pizza parlor. Sometimes a boy or girl invites several friends to their home for an afternoon swimming party or a video game night. These informal group activities away from school will allow you to get to know boys and girls with absolutely no pressure. You can be yourself and have a good time with your friends.

School clubs and activities are another way to enjoy the company of boys and girls in a no-pressure setting. Middle schools typically have several clubs based on student interests: chess club, ecology club, yearbook, newspaper staff, drama, and photography, among others. Everyone there will already have something in common. School dances are also a lot of fun. Plan to go with a group of friends. You can dance and chat and have a great time.

Some students have their first boyfriends or girlfriends while in middle school. Understand that it is very, very, very unlikely that you will marry your middle school sweetheart. Why do we mention this? Because there will be a break-up. It may come in two days or two weeks or two months. But eventually you and your boyfriend/girlfriend will end the relationship. Sometimes those break-ups are calm and sometimes they are dramatic, but there are always hurt feelings. Realize that you will see your "ex" in the hallway every day, and you may even have classes with him or her. The guidance counselor will not change your schedule just because you're in the same class with your former boyfriend or girlfriend.

The best advice is to steer clear of those exclusive, one-to-one relationships. Socialize with boys and girls. Become good friends. There will be time for serious romantic relationships when you're older.

Managing Conflict

Most boys and girls have a few friends that they get along with most of the time. But sometimes we argue with our best friends. That sounds strange, but it's true. It's probably because we spend a lot of time with our friends. They see us when we're at our best, and at our worst. They get the good and the bad. Sometimes we say things we shouldn't, and that can lead to arguments and hurt feelings.

Give It Some Time...

If you're having a conflict with a friend, sometimes it's best just to give it some time. You want to make everything right. You want to act like friends again. But you need to let emotions cool down. You may need to let a few hours, or even a few days pass. This time can be stressful, but it is important.

If you have said or done something to hurt your friend, you should apologize. "I'm sorry. I shouldn't have said that. That's not how I really feel. I don't know what I was thinking." Your friend may put their arm around your shoulder and tell you it's okay, or they may turn around and walk off. But you have apologized. You have done your part. Your friend may need time to think about your apology.

Friendships are emotional, and sometimes our emotions don't do exactly what we want. With time and the willingness to apologize, most friendships can survive an occasional argument or disagreement.

People Who Aren't Your Friends

News Flash! Not everyone will be your friend. You can be friendly and smile and say "hello." But there will be some people who do not want your friendship. You can study and get 100% on your spelling test. You can make all of your free throws on the basketball court. But try as you might, you cannot get everyone to be your friend. That's just a fact of life.

You can't control this. But you *can* control your reaction. How should you react when someone doesn't want to be your friend? Move on. It probably has nothing to do with you, and everything to do with them. Don't waste your time worrying about it. Don't ask them why they don't like you. Don't try to do things to make yourself appealing to them. Just move on. Don't think of it as an insult. Don't make them your enemy. Don't say bad things about them to your friends. Move on. Not everyone will be your friend.

What if someone who is not your friend is trying to cause a conflict with you? Maybe they are saying bad things about you, or picking a fight in the hallway. If possible, ignore their attempts to bait you into a fight. It sounds strange, but some people feel powerful when they challenge other people. Many times if you ignore this person, their taunts will disappear. Rise above it. And it's probably a good idea to tell a teacher or school administrator – not because it's a problem for you, but because you wouldn't want this person to bother anyone else.

Bullying is a serious topic, and most schools have anti-bullying rules in place. If someone is bullying you, report it immediately to a trusted adult.

Friendship will be an important, rewarding part of your middle school years. You will probably keep your friends from elementary school, and make new friends in middle school. Being a friend is a skill that will help you in middle school and in years to come.

Your Turn

Will you go to middle school with people you've known since kindergarten?

Do you have lots of friends, or just a few close friends?

In your own words, what is the difference between an acquaintance and a friend?

Think about one of your close friends. How did that friendship begin? What are some things that you did together that continued that friendship?

Think about a conflict that you had with a friend? How did you solve that conflict? How long did it take?

Make a list of five things that are important if you want to be a good friend.

What characteristics do you look for in a friend?

What characteristics do *you* have that make *you* a good friend?

Chapter 4

Behavior in Middle School

Here's a fact: most middle school students never get in trouble at school. They learn the rules and they follow the rules. They never have to think about it. But because you're getting ready to start middle school, you're probably already thinking about it! Maybe you have ideas of giant, snarling assistant principals lurking in the hall, just waiting to throw you into the middle school dungeon, or some other such silliness.

In this chapter we'll look at behavior and discipline in middle schools. Like most things, it's different from your elementary school. But once you understand the system, you'll feel much better.

Freedom and Self-control

In middle school, students are expected to control their own behavior. By the time you get to middle school, you should know what is acceptable behavior, and what is not. Sometimes elementary students just can't control themselves. They play during class time, run when they should walk, and yell when they should whisper. That's part of the elementary learning process. But it is not expected for middle school students. Middle school students are expected to at least try to control themselves.

Does that mean you can't have fun in middle school? Of course not! Middle school can be a lot of fun. But it's not that silly, out-of-control fun that you often find on an elementary playground. Middle schoolers who act that way in the classroom will be out of place. Students in middle school understand that there's a time and place for work, and a time and place for play. That's what self-control is all about.

Self-control is so important in middle school because you will have much more freedom. Most elementary classes walk from place to place in a straight line. Middle school students navigate the halls as individuals. Elementary students usually sit with their class at lunch, but in many middle schools students can choose their lunchroom tables, or even go outside on a sunny day. Middle school students on the yearbook or newspaper staff may be able to walk around campus without their teacher.

Some middle school students are given additional responsibilities in the classroom or in extra-curricular activities. That's a lot of freedom. And with freedom comes responsibility. In elementary school you are closely supervised every minute of the day. In middle school, behavior boundaries are set, and you are expected to stay within those boundaries.

School Code of Conduct

Almost every middle school has a School Code of Conduct. This code is followed by the administrators, teachers, and students. The School Code of Conduct lists the rules of the school, and describes what happens if students disobey the rules. Your homeroom teacher will probably go over the School Code of Conduct during the first week of school. Here's an example of a section of a Code of Conduct.

Expectation	Violation	First Offense	Subsequent Offenses
Students should be ready for class to begin when the tardy bell rings.	Students are tardy to class.	First and second tardies are handled by the classroom teacher. Verbal warning. Classroom detention may be assigned. Teacher calls the parent after the second tardy.	Third tardy – office referral. Assistant principal will call parent and assign one after school detention (30 minutes.) Fourth tardy – office referral. Assistant principal will call parent and assign two after school detentions (30 minutes.)

So there you have it. That's what happens if a student is tardy to class. The school expects all students to be ready for class to begin when the tardy bell rings. When a student is tardy the first time, he or she will get a warning from the teacher. The teacher may also assign classroom detention for the first or second tardies. The teacher will call the parent and let them know that the student will get an office referral if the tardies continue. If the student is late a third time, the teacher writes an office referral. The

student is sent to the assistant principal's office, and their parent is called. He or she will have to stay after school for 30 minutes (detention.) It's really very simple. No tricks. No surprises. There's the rule, and there's what happens if you break it.

But I Don't Want Detention!

Right now, you may have a queasy feeling in your stomach. You don't want detention, and you don't want the school to call your parents to say you disobeyed the rules.

Well, just follow the rules! Remember the first sentence of this chapter: most students never get in trouble at school. The school gives you every opportunity to follow the rules. The assistant principal would rather not see you in his or her office with a referral.

The expectations (rules) in the School Code of Conduct are there so that school will be safe and orderly. The school administrators – usually the principal and assistant principal – are responsible for enforcing the rules. Nobody likes to think about punishment, but it is part of any Code of Conduct. Most people want to avoid the punishment, so they follow the rules. Without punishment, some people would still follow the rules, but some wouldn't. That's a fact of life.

The School Code of Conduct will include more serious offenses, such as fighting and stealing. There are also more serious punishments, including suspension from school and placement in an alternative school or classroom. These serious things don't happen by accident. Nobody trips in the hallway and falls into a fight. They are the result of some really bad decision making by students. Nobody is happy when students get in trouble.

Before we move on, let's say it one more time: most students never get in trouble at school. Most middle school students have no desire to violate the rules. The Code of Conduct is there as a guide when students make the wrong choice.

School Behavior Problems

In this section, we'll look at some of the most common behavior problems at school, and a few that don't happen very often. Check your school's Code of Conduct for the expectations and consequences at your school.

Classroom Disruption   This is probably the most common discipline problem in middle school. The teacher has planned a lesson and is trying to teach. But one or more students are disrupting the classroom. Maybe they are talking loudly, throwing paper, or acting rudely to their fellow students or the teacher. These are all examples of classroom disruption. Usually a teacher will issue one or two warnings before writing a referral. However, the teacher is responsible for the classroom. If the classroom is disrupted, then the teacher must take action.

Profanity   There are certain words and phrases that you're not allowed to use at school. Sometimes students hear vulgar language and they want to try it in front of their friends at school. This is a very bad idea. You certainly don't want the assistant principal to call your Mom about this!

Skipping Class   Sometimes students decide to skip a full day or a class period. Attendance systems and school video cameras make this a foolish choice. The absence will be noticed.

<u>Public Displays of Affection (PDA)</u>   Most schools have rules about displaying affection to other students. This includes things like holding hands, hugging, and kissing. Believe it or not, in middle school some students want to go around hugging everyone. This seems harmless, but it quickly gets out of control. Some hugs are just a little too friendly. And some people just don't want to be hugged. It sounds pretty foolish to get detention for PDA, but it happens.

<u>Misusing Technology</u>   In middle school, you will probably use computers, tablets, and other technology tools. Schools have rules about how these tools should be used. For example, when you're supposed to be researching your science topic on a school computer, don't try to sneak onto a videogame web site. Students who misuse technology at school can have their technology privileges taken away, in addition to the regular punishment for breaking school rules.

<u>Vandalism</u>   For some reason, some students damage their own school. This includes writing on the walls, purposely destroying something that belongs to the school, or making a mess for the custodians to clean up. Serious cases of vandalism – usually after school hours – can result in police investigation and arrest. Once again, video cameras in the school make it easy to catch the bad guy.

<u>Horseplay</u>   Horseplay is one of those old-fashioned words that describes rowdy playful behavior. There's a time and place for this type of activity – at home, or sometimes in PE class. Horseplay becomes a problem when students play around in the classroom or in the hallway.

Horseplay can also lead to a fight that wasn't supposed to happen. All too often, a boy or girl will playfully touch or nudge one of their friends. That friend may not be in the mood to play, so they push back. Thinking that the game has begun, our friend throws another playful punch. This gets the second person really mad! They're not in a good mood anyway. Before you know it, two good friends are wrestling in the hallway. That's why schools don't like horseplay.

<u>Bullying Behavior</u> Bullying is an important topic in schools. Everyone should be able to go to school without being afraid. Make sure that you're not being a bully.

<u>Stealing</u> Stealing isn't very common in middle school, but it does happen. Most middle school students keep their valuables close to them so they won't get stolen. If you bring your iPad to school and leave it on the cafeteria table after lunch, someone might steal it. Or if you wear an expensive jacket to school and leave it in the gym (instead of your locker) someone might steal it. The smart student leaves his valuable possessions at home.

Temptation

Some people are tempted to steal, and others would never think of taking something that's not theirs. Stealing a pencil is wrong, but the punishment will probably be light. When something valuable is stolen, the school resource officer usually takes over the investigation. That thief will be in serious trouble when caught. If you find yourself tempted to steal, walk away from the setting as quickly as you can!

Remember, "finders keepers" isn't the rule in middle school. If you find something, take it to the front office. When someone loses a valuable item - and you just happen to have it - it's technically not stealing. But you would certainly have a lot of explaining to do!

Fighting   Fighting is actually very rare in middle school, and it is never a wise choice. Students who fight are usually suspended, and may be placed in an alternative classroom or school. If someone threatens you, make sure to tell a school administrator immediately. Administrators take fighting very seriously. They want the school to be a safe place for all students. If you feel angry and you want to fight someone, talk to a teacher, counselor, coach or other trusted adult. Get the help that you need to manage your anger. You can't expect to get along with everyone. Fighting won't solve the problem.

Disrespect and Fighting

When that infrequent fight begins, it is usually because one person feels disrespected or insulted. Those feelings begin with gossip or making rude comments. If you find yourself challenged to a fight, ask yourself if you've done anything to make the other person mad. That doesn't mean that you invited the fight. But it does mean that you should keep gossip and rude comments to yourself.

Drugs, Tobacco, and Alcohol   Taking illegal drugs, using tobacco and drinking alcohol are very foolish behaviors for students. And you certainly wouldn't bring any of these items to school. Sometimes students will bring drugs, tobacco, or alcohol to school to impress their friends. This is a big mistake. Having these items at school usually results in suspension or expulsion. Most teachers and administrators can tell a very sad story on this topic.

Other Disallowed Items   Schools have different rules about what you can bring to school, and what is not allowed. Become familiar with the list of items that you shouldn't bring. Sometimes middle school students bring things to school to show their friends. This is not a good idea. If you want your friends to see your baseball card collection or your new handheld video game, invite them over to your house after school. Many years ago pocketknives were common in schools. Now, they are not allowed in most schools. And in many schools, students aren't allowed to carry pain reliever (aspirin, Tylenol, etc.) or tummy medicine in their pockets or purses.

If you're at school and you discover that you've accidentally brought a disallowed item to school with you, tell your teacher or a school administrator immediately. Typically, they will take the item from you, call your parent, and give the item to your parent after school.

Disrespect to an Adult and Willful Disobedience   The adults are in charge at a school. You should always act respectfully toward your teachers, your counselor, the administrators, and any other adults who work at your school. Be respectful and courteous to the cafeteria workers, the custodians, and the secretaries. Most schools have harsh punishments for students who yell at or argue with an adult.

Willful disobedience means that a student is told to do one thing, and he or she does another. For example, if the PE coach blows the whistle that tells everyone it is time to return to the locker room, but one or two students decide to stay on the field instead, that would be willful disobedience. Here's another example: a student is told to put their cell phone away, but they send text messages in class. A student who is willfully disobedient is saying to the teacher, "You're not in charge, I am!" That will never end well for the student.

<u>Zero Tolerance</u>   Most schools have a few zero tolerance items in the Code of Conduct. "Zero" means "none" and "tolerance" means "accepting something." So, zero tolerance means that the school will not accept this type of behavior one little bit! The action will be swift and severe. Zero tolerance behaviors can include bringing a weapon to school, assaulting a student or teacher, or having drugs or alcohol in your possession. These are very serious offenses – something you would never want to do. These problems are very rare in most middle schools.

As you review this list, you're probably thinking, "Wow! I'd never do any of those things." And you're right. You'll probably never get in trouble at school. Unfortunately, some students continue to make bad choices. In some schools, students with too many office referrals sign a behavior contract that spells out exactly what will happen if the student continues to misbehave. Other schools have a point system, with each referral adding points to the student's total. Students who receive too many points in a semester may be sent to an alternative school for the remainder of the year. That may sound harsh, but we're talking about students who make school dangerous and unpleasant for students and teachers. Most students are able to correct their behavior before it gets that far.

Your school's Code of Conduct will probably be a little bit different, so pay attention when it is presented to you.

Dress Code

Most schools have a Dress Code that students must follow. The Dress Code usually lists the clothes you can and cannot wear. Some Dress Codes also include jewelry and hairstyles.

Your elementary school probably has a Dress Code, but it is usually not an issue. In middle school, students start choosing their own clothes and they want to dress in the current styles. Middle school students usually shop in the juniors department or the young men's department. With all of these changes, it makes sense that middle schools need to have a Dress Code.

The school Dress Code keeps the focus on education, not fashion or bizarre dress. If a student comes to school with a spiked haircut dyed hot pink, there probably won't be much learning going on in that classroom. Everybody will be staring at the hairstyle. Some t-shirts have words or pictures that aren't appropriate for school. Expect these items to be covered in your school Dress Code.

During the middle school years, the human body changes and develops. Boys and girls notice these changes, and become very interested in members of the opposite sex. So, if a student is wearing clothing that reveals too much, it may be hard for some students to keep their minds on the lesson. You can giggle if you want to, but that's a fact of life.

Dress Code?

Because everyone's body develops on a different time schedule, an outfit that is perfectly fine for one student will be too revealing for another student. And the shorts that were the right length at the beginning of the school year may be too short and too tight in the springtime.

Shopping Challenges

Teachers and administrators understand that following the Dress Code can be challenging when shopping for new clothes. Girl's short pants found in popular stores are often shorter than the Dress Code allows. Fashionable jeans may have rips and tears, and some schools don't allow that. Buying appropriate clothing is usually easier for boys.

Some schools have very strict Dress Codes, and others are more lax. Your school may allow short skirts, ripped jeans, purple hair, and lip piercings (ouch!) Or your school may require uniforms. Most schools are somewhere in between.

Dress Code violations are usually handled as discipline issues. You really don't want a detention for wearing shorts that are too short or coloring your hair green. Some schools send students to an in-school suspension room until their parent can bring appropriate clothes. Other schools provide sweatpants and t-shirts for Dress Code violators to wear. The smart thing to do is to learn about your school's Dress Code and follow it.

In the Discipline Office

We've said several times in this chapter that you will probably never get in trouble in middle school. But for just a moment, imagine that you forgot to study for your math test (mistake #1) so you decided to skip math class today (mistake #2.) You were sitting on the bench in front of the school library when the assistant principal approached you and said, "Where are you supposed to be?" Because there is simply not a good answer for that question, you find yourself sitting in front of the assistant principal's desk, in the "hot seat."

What should you do?

Don't make mistake #3. Mistake #3 would be to lie to the assistant principal!

Any lie that you could tell the assistant principal could easily be discovered. There's just no good reason for you to be in front of the school library when you're supposed to be in math class. It doesn't make sense. And if it doesn't make sense, it's probably not true. A lie usually gets a person in more trouble, not less.

Telling the Truth

Trying to get out of trouble is human nature. We all make mistakes. When faced with these mistakes, our first instinct is to explain them away. But as we get older, we realize that telling the truth is almost always the best thing to do.

Telling the truth about a mistake that you made can be hard. It means that you will probably be punished for that mistake. It also will show your parents, teachers, and administrators that you understand your mistake, you've learned from it, and you won't do it again. That's the message that adults want and need to hear. So, if you find yourself in trouble at school, recognize your mistake, own it, and tell the truth.

Apologizing

Apologizing for your behavior mistake is also important. It helps to ease the conflict between you and the other people involved. Let's say you're in trouble for class disruption. You made this great paper airplane, and you just can't wait to see how it flies. So, you launch it right in the middle of history class. The plane spirals perfectly around the classroom before landing at the feet of the teacher. Everyone (except the teacher) laughs, and it takes a few minutes to get the class back on track. This is classroom disruption. Everybody saw it. Everybody knows it. And now you're in the office.

If this is your first discipline referral you'll probably get a 30-minute afternoon detention. The administrator will call your parents and explain what happened. The administrator will talk to you for a few minutes. He wants to make sure you understand that he doesn't expect this type of behavior to happen again. As an intelligent person, you assure him it will not.

You also owe the teacher an apology. Don't wrap your apology in an excuse ("I thought you'd like my airplane.") Don't blame your misbehavior on somebody else ("Dennis said I had a great airplane.") It was your mistake. Own it. Apologize. Look the teacher in the eye, and say something like this:

> *"Mr. Lewis, I am very sorry I interrupted your class. I shouldn't have thrown that paper airplane. I feel really bad about it. It won't happen again."*

It's really pretty simple. Whether you planned it or not, throwing that paper airplane was very disrespectful to the teacher. Apologizing lets the teacher know that you have learned from your mistake.

Three More Tips

Here are three more ideas about school behavior and discipline.

First, understand that there's a difference between classroom correction and punishment. If a teacher believes that you are talking too much to the person sitting beside you, they will probably move you to a different seat. That's the teacher's choice. You're not in trouble. The teacher is trying to keep you from  getting in trouble. Or maybe your behavior needs improvement and the teacher talks to you about it after class. That doesn't mean you're in trouble. The teacher is simply giving you a warning. For less serious behavior problems, most teachers will call a parent before writing a referral. Once again, the teacher is trying to correct the problem before it becomes something serious.

 Sure, it's hard to believe that your teacher is actually helping you when your parents get a phone call, or you have to stay a few minutes after class. But really, they are doing you a favor. They are letting you know that you've reached the limit of acceptable behavior.

Number two: if you break the rules, don't try to avoid the punishment. The punishment is there to help you remember not to make the same mistake again. Punishment also discourages other students from breaking the rules. Some students want their parents to get them excused from the punishment. This is a big mistake. Very few parents and almost no administrators would agree to that. And the school has to treat everyone the way they treat you. Do administrators make mistakes? Absolutely. And if you know that you are being punished unfairly you should talk to your parents. But if you broke the rules, accept the punishment.

Finally, understand that some students get caught breaking the rules. Other students break the same rules, but they don't get caught. That's not a good thing, but it happens. The fact that some rule-breakers escape punishment doesn't excuse your referral. In a perfect world, everyone who breaks the rules would get caught. Realistically, some rule-breakers go unpunished. Your concern should be for your own behavior, and not anyone else's.

Remember, most students never get in trouble at school. It is important for everyone to know the rules and follow them. The School Code of Conduct makes school safe and orderly. When the Code of Conduct is followed, school is a place where you can learn and have fun, too.

Your Turn

Middle school has more freedom, and more responsibility. What are some of the middle school freedoms that you're looking forward to?

Look at the behaviors in the chart below. Write what you think should be the punishment. Then, read your middle school's Code of Conduct and find out what the real punishment is.

Misbehavior	What I think will happen	Our School Code of Conduct
Class disruption		
Skipping a class		
Bringing tobacco to school		

Get a copy of the middle school Dress Code. What are some things listed that you want to pay special attention to?

Part of the paper airplane story says, "It was your mistake. Own it. Apologize." In your own words, what does it mean to "own" your mistake? Why is this important?

Chapter 5

Attendance

You're ready for middle school, so you probably know all about attendance. Simply stated, if you want to learn, you need to attend school.   Students who are absent a lot usually have a hard time keeping up with the class.   Of course, sometimes you're dealing with health issues or your family takes an emergency trip. You miss school and you really can't help it.   But whenever possible you should attend school. You know that.

That same concept is true in middle school too.   In this short chapter we'll review some attendance basics.   We'll also see how middle school attendance is just a little different.

It's important to learn about the attendance policy at school.   Your school's attendance policy will probably have information about excused absences, tardies, and make-up work.   Every school is a little bit different, so make sure you follow the attendance rules at your school.

Absences and Tardies

When you are absent you do not attend school the entire day.   When you are tardy, you are late.   That's pretty simple in elementary school, but it's a little more complicated in middle school.   Let's say your school starts at 8:00 AM, but for some reason you don't get there until 9:00 AM. Maybe you overslept, or you had an early-morning dentist check-up. At 9:00 AM you sign-in at the front desk and begin your school day.

But you go to second period. You were tardy to school, but you were absent from first period. You missed the entire class. Maybe you missed a new topic, a test, or an important science experiment. Whatever it was, you missed it! In elementary school you could just take your seat and pick-up with the rest of the class. Your elementary teacher could probably provide the assignments later on that day. Middle school is different. You could visit your first period teacher later in the day, or maybe get the assignment from your friend.

A Big Mistake!

Here's a tip: never say to a teacher, "I was absent. Did I miss anything?" The answer is obvious: of course you missed something! Instead, ask the teacher if it's possible to get the classwork so that you can do it for homework. This will make the teacher happy!

Excused Absences and Unexcused Absences

Your school will have two categories of absences: excused absences and unexcused absences. Make sure you know what type of absence goes in each category. When you are sick, that's usually an excused absence, especially if your doctor or your parent writes a note. If you go shopping with your grandmother, that will probably be an unexcused absence.

There's a difference between a reason and an excuse. Sometimes you have a good reason for being absent or tardy, but it's really not an excuse. Here's an example: let's say that your family decides to go out to eat for breakfast on Wednesday morning. Because it's All-You-Can-Eat Pancake Day, you miss all of first period, and about half of second period. Is there a reason you were absent? Sure! You were eating pancakes! But that's probably not an excuse a school would accept. Every school is a little bit different when it comes to excuses, so make sure you know your school's policy.

Problems with Unexcused Absences

Most schools limit the number of unexcused absences you can have. Sometimes there are penalties when you have too many unexcused absences. Some schools do not allow you to make up any work that you missed if your absence is unexcused. If you're on a sports team, your coach may have rules about unexcused absences. You may even be denied credit for a class if you have too many unexcused absences. That means that you would have to re-take the entire class! Schools take attendance very seriously. Before you decide to be absent for no good reason, think about the consequences of an unexcused absence.

Pre-arranged Absences

Sometimes you know in advance that you are going to be absent. Maybe you have a medical issue, and you need to get minor surgery. Maybe your family reunion is in another state the 2nd week of October, and your family plans to attend. Or maybe you're on the soccer team and you're playing in the state tournament. If you are going to be absent for more than a day or two, the school may ask you to complete a pre-arranged absence form.

Most pre-arranged absence forms are pretty simple. You and your parents fill-out the dates you plan to be absent, and your parents sign the form. Then, you take the form to each of your teachers and they initial it. Most teachers will write down the assignments that you will miss during your absences. You can usually work on your assignments if you have time during your absence. That way, you won't be so far behind when you return.

If You're Absent, Tardy, or Signing-Out

Some students have perfect attendance, and they are never tardy! But most students are absent or tardy at least once or twice during the school year. Your school has procedures for returning to school after you've been absent or tardy.

Most schools ask you to go to the office before first period when you return after an absence. (Some schools take care of this during homeroom, before first period.) The secretary will take your excuse note and give you an admittance slip. You take the admittance slip to every class during the day and show it to your teachers. This slip lets your teachers know if your absence was excused or unexcused.

If you're tardy to school, your parent will probably have to come into the school building and sign the sign-in sheet. The secretary will give you a tardy pass to take to your first period class.

If you have to leave school during the school day, make sure to go through the front office. Your parent will probably need to come inside the office and sign you out. Some students make the mistake of just walking out to the parking lot when it's time for their dentist appointment. This is a mistake, because the school needs to know when students leave campus.

Your school policies may be a little different. Make sure you pay attention during your middle school orientation, or whenever the information is presented. Middle schools keep careful attendance records.

Make-up Work

When you miss a class, you need to ask your teacher about the assignments you missed. An absence – either excused, unexcused, or pre-arranged – does not mean that you are excused from the assignments. You will probably have only a few days to turn in the work. The grade will be a zero in the grade book until the work is turned in.

Make-up Work

In middle school, make-up work is the student's responsibility, not the teacher's. Asking the teacher is usually better than asking a friend, because the make-up assignment may be slightly different than the assignment given in class. You should ask about the make-up work on the first day that you return to school.

Leaving During the School Day

Sometimes students have to leave school during the school day. As mentioned earlier, you always want to go through the front office when leaving school during the school day. Your parent will probably need to come inside the school and sign you out. Here are some things to consider when leaving school during the day.

Missing 30 Minutes of School...

Missing thirty minutes of school is missing half of a class period. In elementary school, you could probably miss thirty minutes and quickly catch-up when you return. Not so in middle school. That's the same as missing half of your language arts or science class. Middle school teachers usually fill each class period with important lessons.

Sometimes you can't avoid checking out of school during the day. Just realize that you'll be missing all or most of a class, and you'll need to get the make-up work when you return.

Vary Appointment Times

Some students need to check out during the day several times during the month. This is often for medical reasons, such as allergy shots, physical therapy, or orthodontist appointments. If that's you, ask your parents if you can have the appointments at different times during the day.

For instance, let's say you injured your knee playing soccer (ouch!) You have a physical therapy appointment twice a week for the next month. Just to keep it simple, your physical therapist always schedules the therapy on Tuesdays and Thursdays at 10 AM. So, every Tuesday and Thursday you'll miss all of math class and half of history class. That's another big ouch! See if your parents can schedule your appointments for different times. It may be possible, or it may not be. But it would keep you from missing so many days in one class. That's something to think about.

Electives are Important, Too!

Some students will always schedule their time away from school during their elective periods. In elementary school, this is probably a good idea. Elementary art, music, and PE classes are important, but it's okay if you miss an assignment or two. Middle school elective classes may have projects, tests, and homework. This work will need to be made-up when you return to school.

Ending the School Day Early

Sometimes students want to end the school day early. They ask their parents to check them out of school 15 or 20 minutes before the school day ends. Once again, this is usually a mistake. You may be tempted to leave school early to get ready for softball practice, or to help your mom with errands. These absences add up. You really can't expect to pass your last class of the day if you're absent half the time. Once again, this is a difference between elementary school and middle school. In elementary school, the last 20 minutes of the day may be spent cleaning-up, packing book bags, and stuffing pages in the take-home folder. In middle school, the last twenty minutes of your last class are very important. If at all possible, plan to stay at school all day, every day.

Attendance is very important in middle school. Your teachers plan class periods with lessons, activities, and tests. And you'll have several class periods every day.

Come to school every day that you are able to get the most out of middle school.

Your Turn

Imagine your friend is 30 minutes late to school every day. What advice would you give him or her about ways to get to school on time?

At your elementary or middle school, what happens when a student has an unexcused absence?   Can the student make-up the missed work?

At your middle school, what will you need to do when you return to school after you are absent for a day?

Chapter 6

Using Technology

Most middle school students know a lot about technology. You probably know how to use a desktop computer, a laptop computer, a tablet, and a smartphone. You might use technology to talk with your friends, play games, listen to music, and create pictures and videos. Most people use some type of computer technology every day. In this chapter, we'll look at how technology is used in middle school.

At school you will use technology for education. That sounds simple, but it's really hard for some students to understand. Think about it for a minute – when you open your laptop computer or pick up your tablet, what do you do? Check Facebook? Use a messaging app? Play a game? As long as you're "being good" there's nothing really wrong with any of those things. But you will need to make an adjustment when you get to middle school.

When a middle school teacher hands you a tablet or takes you to a computer lab, they have something that they want you to do. They may want you to open an app on the solar system, or go to a web site to watch a science experiment. Maybe they'll ask you to type your essay, build a PowerPoint presentation, or learn some words in Spanish. Unfortunately, some students go straight to a game site or log-on to Facebook as soon as they see technology. And usually, they get in trouble for it. Wait for instructions, listen carefully, and use the technology in the way the teacher tells you. In school, technology is a tool, not a toy.

Follow the Rules

When you use technology at school, plan to be responsible and follow the rules. Students can be very creative when using technology. That becomes a problem if you violate school rules. Some students get their first (and only) office referral for using their cell phone in class, or sneaking to a game web site in the computer lab. Don't make that mistake.

Computer Resources

The computers in your middle school are only part of the technology system. The school also provides resources to help you use the technology.

Computer classes

Middle school students can take classes about using computers. The exploratory wheel class described in Chapter 1 will probably have a computer section. A wheel computer class could include keyboarding, computer research, Internet safety, and office software (Word, PowerPoint, etc.) Many middle schools offer advanced computer classes. These classes include computer applications, web page design, digital photography, computer programming, and robotics.

In middle school, you can expect to have lessons on Internet safety. Some schools invite guest speakers to talk about being safe online. The school resource officer knows a lot about this topic. Students from a local high school might visit the middle school to share their experiences.

Internet Safety – Worth a Listen

Internet safety is very important. Social media apps like Facebook can be a lot of fun. But sometimes people use computer technology to harm other people. When Internet safety lessons are presented, listen carefully and ask questions.

Online Resources

Most middle schools give their students access to some amazing online resources. You may be able to use these web sites at home, too. Online resources could include:

- An online encyclopedia
- A web-site with magazine and newspaper articles
- Animations and instructional videos (BrainPop, etc.)
- Your school's online library catalog
- A web-site for downloading and reading eBooks and audiobooks
- Your textbooks online.

Your teacher or library media specialist will give you the user name and password for each online resource.

Teacher Web Pages

Some of your teachers will have classroom web pages. Each web page will have information about the class, links to important web sites, and the teacher's e-mail address. Some teachers post their assignments on a web page, and you can upload your work to the web site when you're finished. You teacher could even make videos to help you with your homework.

If all this is a bit confusing, don't worry. If a teacher expects you to use their web page, they'll show you how. And if you don't have a computer at home, that's okay too. Just don't be surprised if you end your first week of middle school with a list of web sites about your classes.

Online Grade Book

Almost all middle schools use an Internet-based grade book. Students (and their parents) can see their grades at any time. You can understand exactly how you're doing in every class. You can also see if you're missing any assignments. Check your grades at least once a week. There's really no reason to be surprised at report card time.

Using School-owned Technology

Desktop computers, laptop computers, and tablets are pretty common in middle school. Middle schools are also wired to access the Internet. Some schools connect to the Internet wirelessly. Teachers and administrators can share files from one computer to another.

Acceptable Use Policy

With so much money spent on technology, it makes sense to have some rules about how school technology is used. That set of rules is called an Acceptable Use Policy.

In Chapter 4 we talked about the Code of Conduct. You probably remember that the Code of Conduct is a list of rules and the consequences for breaking those rules. The Acceptable Use Policy is a Code of Conduct for technology.

The Acceptable Use Policy tells you what you can and can't do with a school-owned computer. Here are some things that might be included in an Acceptable Use Policy:

- Installing programs on a school computer
- Changing the settings on a school computer
- Using a school computer to send e-mail
- Using a school computer to bully another student
- Copying programs, files, and games using a school computer.

Of course, there are penalties for breaking the rules. A student who violates the Acceptable Use Policy might not get to use a computer for a week, a month, or the entire year. Some schools treat breaking the computer rules just like any discipline referral.

The Acceptable Use Policy is there so that the computers will always be up and running, and so that nobody gets in trouble using the computer. Your teachers will go over the Acceptable Use Policy early in the school year. If you have any questions, make sure to ask. You will probably sign the policy, and a copy will be kept in the office.

Using Technology for the Intended Purpose

We talked about this earlier in the chapter, but it's important enough to repeat. When your teacher gives you access to technology, they will have something for you to do. A teacher will never take you to the computer lab so that you can play video games or check your Facebook page. Some students are very tempted to use the computer for something else. Be very careful. Most computer labs have software that lets the teacher see anyone's computer. And the computer network manager can easily see which web sites you visit.

It might be hard, but you can manage these distractions. Keep your mind on the assignment. Computer games are fun, but they're not worth losing your school computer privileges.

Changing Computer Settings

When you use a computer or tablet at school, you're supposed to leave it exactly like you found it. Don't change any of the settings on the computer.

Why Can't I Change the Computer Settings?

With just a little bit of knowledge, a person can make a lot of changes to the appearance of a computer. Screen savers, desktop pictures, cursors (pointers) and fonts are among those changes. But most Acceptable Use Policies have rules against this. The school's computers are set to work for everyone. Changing the settings can make the computer run slower, and make programs crash.

If you need to make changes so that you can use the computer better, then ask the teacher. Otherwise, don't change the computer settings.

Computer Labs and Classrooms

Middle school classes use computers for research and project creation. Your language arts teacher could assign a report on a well-known poet. In history class you might work on a PowerPoint about a battle of the American Revolution. Your science project group may need some information for an experiment about pollution. You will go to a computer lab with your class to complete all of these tasks.

Computer Labs

A computer lab is a room with enough computers to host an entire class. Computer labs often have a printer, a digital camera, and a scanner. Teachers schedule their classes to meet in the computer lab for an assignment using technology. Your class may meet in the computer lab for several days if you are working on a big project. Your middle school may have one, two, or several computer labs.

Some schools buy computer labs on wheels. Twenty-five or more laptop computers are stored on a cart, and the cart is rolled to a classroom. The cart is also a charging station. The rolling computer lab may also have Internet access and a printer. Maybe your class used a rolling computer lab in elementary school. A computer lab on wheels is a good choice when a school wants to add a computer lab, but there's not an available classroom.

Computer Classrooms

Some classes meet every day in a computer lab. As you've probably guessed, these are computer classes! If you're in a class learning to create documents or build web pages, then you need a computer every day.

One-to-One Program

Some schools issue a laptop computer or a tablet to each student at the beginning of the year. This is called a one-to-one program, because there is one computer for every student. The student is responsible for the computer for the entire school year. These schools don't really need computer labs, because every student has a computer every day.

A Big Responsibility

Getting your own laptop sounds exciting, but it's a big responsibility. A student in a one-to-one program has to make sure his or her laptop is in class and the battery is charged. It's also one more thing to keep up with. You certainly wouldn't want to lose or drop the school's computer. If your school has a one-to-one program, make sure you take care of the computer.

Bringing Your Own Technology

You may own a laptop computer, a tablet, and a smartphone. Can you bring these devices to school and use them? The answer to that question depends on your school. In some schools, students can use their own technology and even log-on to the school's wireless Internet. In other schools this is strictly forbidden. Of course, your school will tell you the policy during the first week of the school year.

Even if you can take your technology to school, you may choose to leave those things at home. The school will provide the computers that you need. Any expensive item that you bring to school could get stolen or damaged, and you wouldn't want that to happen.

Make sure that your personal gadgets don't get you in trouble. In middle school it's up to you to stay focused on school. For most students, walking around with a tablet or smartphone is a big distraction. School time is not Facebook time or video game time or Netflix time. If your schoolwork suffers, or if you start getting in trouble, then it's best just to leave the tablet or smartphone at home.

Using a Camera at School

Digital cameras are everywhere, and chances are you have used one. We have cameras on our phones, our tablets, and our computers. Your middle school will have rules about where you can and cannot use a digital camera at school. If you have a digital camera at school, make sure you follow the rules and behave responsibly.

You may think it's great fun to walk around between classes snapping pictures of your friends. But your friends might not want their pictures taken that day. Your friends will just ask you to erase the picture. Strangers would take your photography a little more seriously.

Think Before You Snap!

Really, most people want to have control over who has their picture. You probably wouldn't want just anyone to have a picture of you. That picture could be sent via text or e-mail, or even posted on the Internet. You also want to make sure you don't use your camera to bully or make fun of other students. And never, ever, EVER take a picture in the school bathroom, even if it's just a selfie in the bathroom mirror. That situation can be a real disaster!

School is supposed to be a safe place. For that reason, most schools have rules about taking pictures at school and posting them on the Internet. So, if you take pictures at school, you shouldn't plan to post them on Facebook or any other web site. School is not a public place, like a park or a shopping mall. If you are allowed to use a camera at school, be responsible. If you aren't allowed, then follow the rules and practice your photography away from school.

Texting at School

Some schools allow students to bring cell phones to school. Other schools forbid it. Sometimes students have to leave the phone in their locker. It all depends on your school's rules. Learn your school's cell phone rules during the first week of school.

Some students try to text or instant message their friends during class. This is a bad idea. Even if your school allows texting, you shouldn't text during class. Any teacher would consider texting in class disrespectful. The teacher will talk to your parents, and you may be without your phone for a while.

Technology is an important tool for students in middle school. You can use technology to research topics and create excellent presentations. You may also get to take some advanced computer classes. Remember the reason for using technology in school: education. Don't get distracted. Stay focused on the assignment, and you will be successful in middle school.

Your Turn

What types of technology (computers, tablets, etc.) do you use regularly?

What are some of the things that you do with technology?

Are you interested in taking computer classes in middle school? If so, what would you like to learn?

Why shouldn't you change the settings (wallpaper, screensaver, etc.) on a computer in the school computer lab?

Are you allowed to bring a cell phone to your middle school? If so, when and where are you allowed to use it?

When would it be a bad idea to take a picture of someone at school?

Chapter 7

Getting Organized and Staying Informed

I lost my...

I left my...

I didn't know...

Many sentences spoken by middle schoolers begin with those words.

I lost my jacket!

I left my lunchbox in the computer lab!

I didn't know I have a science test today!

I lost my locker combination!

I left my band instrument on the bus!

I didn't know soccer tryouts were yesterday!

You probably didn't feel good reading those sentences. Maybe you've said those words, or something like them, recently. Losing things, forgetting things, and missing important events can make you feel really crummy. In this chapter, we'll look at ways to get organized and stay informed while you're in middle school.

Be Proactive

If you want to get organized and stay informed in middle school, you need to be proactive. What does it mean to be proactive? It means that you're going to take an active role in your life. You're not just going to sit back and let things happen to you. You're going to think about the future and what might happen tomorrow, next week, and next month. You take care of business today, and plan ahead for tomorrow.

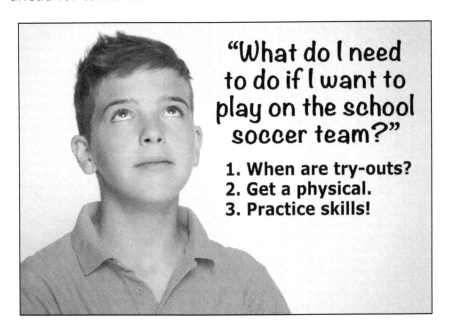

"What do I need to do if I want to play on the school soccer team?"

1. When are try-outs?
2. Get a physical.
3. Practice skills!

Here's an example of a proactive attitude. Let's say you want to try out for the soccer team. You ask your PE teacher, and find out that soccer is a winter sport. Tryouts will be sometime in November. So, you open your planner and write "Soccer Tryouts?" in the space for the last week of October. You go to the school web site and find the soccer web page. You learn that everyone who plays soccer needs to have a current physical on file. (A physical is an examination by a doctor.) So, you ask your parents to schedule a doctor's appointment for your physical. You bookmark the soccer web page on your computer. You practice your soccer skills a few times a week, so that you'll be ready for tryouts. You watch the bulletin boards, and listen to the announcements each day. Sure enough, at the end of October you hear an announcement about soccer tryouts. You are ready!

How would this work for someone who is not proactive? This student doesn't ask the coach about soccer, and never checks the web site. They talk during morning announcements, and never check the school bulletin boards. They miss the first day of tryouts, and show up for the second day after they hear their friends talk about it. But they can't participate because they haven't had their physical exam. This student wants to play soccer, just like our proactive student. But because he is passive about the whole experience, he has to wait until next year.

Anticipate, Ask, and Act!

As we've said throughout this book, middle school students need to be responsible. Being proactive works in many middle school situations. We'll look at some of them later in this chapter. Just remember – anticipate, ask, and act!

Dealing with Stress

Before we go any further, don't think that you have to be perfect. Everybody makes mistakes. Everybody learns along the way. If you lose your jacket, you will probably find it in lost-and-found. If you forget your locker combination, it's probably written down somewhere. If you forget about a test, just do your best and ask about extra credit. Things have a way of working out when you really try.

Your first week of middle school will probably be the hardest. It will get easier. Before you know it, changing classes five or six times a day will be normal. You'll open your locker without even thinking about it. You won't forget your math homework (again.) You will adjust.

It might be a big challenge, but remember to learn from your mistakes. Don't panic when you can't find your history classroom. Don't scream and cry if you can't get your locker open. Just take a deep breath and ask a teacher for help. Stress just gives you something else to deal with. Focus on the solution, and be proactive in the future. The school gets a new group of students every year. You're not the first person to forget your pencil. Teachers and administrators will help you.

Organizing Your Schoolwork

In middle school, it's up to you to organize your schoolwork. Here are some things that you will need to organize.

- Making sure you have the right books and folders for each class
- Making sure you take home the items you will need for homework
- Giving yourself time to work on long-term class projects
- Writing down homework assignments, and upcoming test dates
- Packing your book bag for school each day
- Gathering items you need for band and sports teams.

You will be responsible for all of these things, and more.

Your Planner is Your Friend

Most middle schools ask students to buy a planner. A planner is a calendar about the size of a spiral notebook. It has plenty of space for you to write down homework assignments, sports practices, and club meetings. Wouldn't it be great to have a friend who would always remind you of important things you need to do? That "friend" is your planner.

Some teachers post the weekly assignments on the board, and the students copy the assignments in their planners on Monday. You should also open your planner during morning announcements. You can write down club meetings, team practices, and upcoming dances. Sometimes students also write down non-school events in their planners – things like vacations, parties, and holidays. Every day you can look at your planner to see the important things in your future.

Completing Your Assignments

Your planner will help you keep track of your assignments, but it's up to you to complete them. As a middle schooler, you will be responsible for your assignments.

How much time will your homework take? The answer: as long as it takes to do it correctly and completely. Sometimes a few math problems may take five or ten minutes to complete. Your language arts teacher may assign thirty minutes of reading. You may need to study 45 minutes for a very  important history test. You may spend an hour or more working on your science fair project. Some nights you may have no homework at all. That's why it's important to manage your assignments, and be prepared to work as long as it takes.

Try to avoid distractions while doing your homework. Let's imagine you have ten math problems for homework. This should take you about 20 minutes. So, you get out your math book, and grab a piece of paper and a pencil. And you turn the TV to a music video channel. And you open the messaging app on your phone. And you log-in to Facebook on your tablet.

Before you know it, it's an hour later and you've done exactly one math problem. "I can't believe this math is taking so long!" You've probably figured out that there are just too many distractions. Limit your distractions, focus on the assignments, and your homework will go much faster.

When you have a long-term assignment, try to begin working as soon as you can. Some students make the mistake of trying to do everything at the last minute. Let's say it's Wednesday. Your history teacher tells you that by next Monday you should read Chapter 12 and answer the questions at the end of the chapter. Okay – you can do that over the weekend, right? But maybe your friend invites you to spend the night Friday night, and your Mom takes you shopping on Saturday. Then your grandfather calls on Sunday and says he has two tickets to the ball game – do you want to go? Too bad you have that history chapter to read. Start each assignment early, and work at a steady pace.

Finally, if you don't finish an assignment, plan to make it up as soon as possible. Don't expect to be excused. Most teachers will let you turn in one or two late assignments. But the solution is to get more organized, manage your distractions, start early, and work until you're finished.

Organizing Your Stuff

You will probably have more things to keep up with in middle school. You will have a textbook and a folder for most of your classes. You may also have a band instrument, clothes for PE, and a jacket or sweater. In elementary school, you probably had the same desk all day. You could keep all of your school supplies and books in that desk. In middle school, you may have six different desks, and you won't be able to store items there. So, it's up to you to know what you need and keep those items under your control.

Consistency

Consistency is important. Consistency means doing things the same way every time. Find a good place to store your belongings, put them there every time, and you'll always know where they are. Where's your jacket? It's in your locker. You always put it there. Where's your math homework? It's in the front pocket of your math folder. That's where you always put your homework when you finish. Be consistent!

Here are some tips about organizing the things you take to school.

Organize Your Homework and Book Bag

Homework is the item lost the most often. When you finish your homework, put it in the same place every time – for example the front pocket of your folder. Do the same for every class. That way, you're not scrambling through your book bag desperately trying to find your homework. And remember to clean out your folders every few weeks. It will be harder to find your current assignments if you keep all of your old papers in your folders.

You should pack your book bag the night before school, and put it where you will see it in the morning. Some students put their book bags beside their bedroom door, beside the front door, or at the end of the couch. This is better than trying to pack your book bag in the morning, when the family is rushing around getting ready for school or work.

Take Just What You Need

If you need something, take it to school. If you don't need it, leave it home. The more things you take to school, the greater the chance of losing something. Don't stuff your book bag with things you don't need for school.

Your Locker

Because you'll be changing classes all day, your locker is very important. Keep your books, folders, jacket, gym shoes, and extra school supplies in your locker. Don't stuff your locker with things you don't need. You will probably spend only a few minutes each day at your locker. Keep it neat, organized, and free of trash. You have just a few minutes between classes. You need to be able to open your locker, grab what you need, and move on to your next class.

If your school is small and your locker is near the middle of campus, you may be able to go to your locker several times a day. Students at larger schools need to plan their locker visits around their schedules. For example, you might be able to go to your locker before school, after third period, and at the end of the day. At each locker visit you get what you need for the upcoming classes, or for homework.

At some schools students bring their own locks. At other schools, the locks are built-in to the locker and the school will tell you the combination. Either way, you need to write down your locker combination somewhere. You will remember it...until you forget it. Your planner is a good place to write your locker combination. But don't make it obvious. Don't write "My Locker Combination: 17-01-16" in the front of your planner. Instead, write the combination in a special place that you will remember (maybe your birthday in your planner.) That way, your locker combination is safe, even if you lose your planner.

School Supplies

You will probably want to keep some extra school supplies at school. It's nice to have an extra pencil or pen in your book bag, and two or three more in your locker.

Just remember, don't overstuff your locker, and don't buy more than you need at the store. One of your teachers may ask you to buy a yellow highlighter for class.

So – buy a yellow highlighter and bring it to school. Maybe you buy two yellow highlighters in case the first one runs out of ink, or your friend forgets his highlighter. Don't buy the 12-pack of highlighters in every color imaginable and bring them all to school. You probably won't need your own stapler, hole-punch or tape dispenser either. (Yes, some students bring these to school!) Don't be a school supply show-off. Bring what you need, and leave the rest at home.

Jackets and Shoes

Of course, it all depends on the weather at your school, but you probably won't need your jacket all day long. Keep your jacket in your locker during the day. That way, even if you forget to take it home you will know that it is locked-up safe and sound. And it's also a good idea to keep your gym shoes in your locker, rather than carry them around to your classes. You can go to your locker before PE class if you need to get your shoes.

Keep Up With Your Things

Jackets and shoes can be very expensive. Someone worked hard to buy those things for you. Take care of your jackets, sweaters, sweatshirts, and gym shoes.

Lost and Found

Even if you bring only what you need and carefully manage your things, you might lose something at school. Most middle schools have a lost-and-found box for items that are left in class, the cafeteria, the gym, or in the hallways. This should be the first place you look if you can't find something that you lose at school. If the item that you lose is very valuable or unique – like a band instrument or cell phone – you should also tell someone in the school office. The people who work there will be on the lookout for your lost item. When you find your lost item, ask yourself why you lost it, and make a plan for keeping up with it in the future.

Staying Informed

In middle school, there are a lot of clubs, activities, and sports teams. If you have any interest in these, you will need to stay informed. Of course, you also need to know about assignments and projects in each of your classes. Here are some tips about getting the information you need in middle school.

Class Assignments

Most middle school teachers write their assignments on the board each week. Some teachers also have a class web page that lists the assignments. During the first week of school learn where your teachers write their assignments. Copy the assignments in your planner.

Morning Announcements

 The morning announcements are very important in middle school. (Some schools make morning announcements over the intercom, and other schools have a TV news program.) If you want to know what's going on at school, listen to the announcements. You can write important dates in your planner.

Morning announcements could include:

- Club meetings
- Sports tryouts
- Band and chorus rehearsal
- School events, like dances and parties
- Important announcements about classes
- Canceled meetings or activities.

Some schools also make afternoon announcements. These announcements are often about changes, such as practices that have been canceled, or a change in the location of a club meeting.

School Web Site

Most schools have a web site with important information. Find the web pages for your clubs and teams, and check them frequently. You can also use the school web site to find out about team tryouts and special events.

Learn Locations

When you have the time, do a little "research" on the different places at your school. Most middle schools have maps. Take a few minutes and learn where the office, the library, the cafeteria, and the bathrooms are on campus. A school map can help you get the big picture of middle school. If you go to a small school, this may not be an issue. But if you'll be at a large middle school, it's very important to learn your way around.

We started this chapter with three phrases: *I lost my, I left my*, and *I didn't know*. Be proactive in organizing your schoolwork and your personal belongings. Listen to the morning announcements and check the school web site. Learn everything you can about your school. A student who avoids *I lost my, I left my*, and *I didn't know* will be much happier in middle school.

Your Turn

You find out that your school has a photography contest every year. Because you are proactive, what are some things you would do if you want to enter?

Have you ever used a planner before? If so, what did you write in it? Why will it be important to use a planner in middle school?

Where will you put your book bag in the evening so that you won't have to search for it in the morning?

What are some things that students bring to school that they don't really need?

Ask a teacher or current middle school student: how does the middle school provide information to students?

Does your middle school have any Open Houses or summer programs for incoming students?

Chapter 8

Clubs, Sports, and Activities

Most middle school students enjoy one or more clubs, sports, or activities. These are called extra-curricular activities because they aren't part of your school day. Clubs, sports, and other school activities usually meet or hold practice after the school day ends. Sometimes they meet before school or at lunchtime.

There are many reasons for joining a club, a team, or participating in school activities. The main reason is to have fun! Extra-curricular activities give you a chance to explore something you're interested in. You can also make friends who like the same things. Middle school may be your first chance to join a group or team. Members of clubs and sports teams learn skills like teamwork and leadership. You've probably already thought about clubs, teams, and activities that you'd like to join.

Clubs

Middle schools have many clubs that you can join. Although every middle school is different, most offer clubs like the ones described in this chapter.

Interest Clubs

Some of the most popular middle school clubs are based on things students are interested in. Examples of clubs based on interest include the chess club, the art club, the photography club, and the science club. These clubs usually meet after school and learn more about their topics. Some clubs have guest speakers, take field trips, and have parties. The chess club would probably have a tournament, and the art club would give you a chance to work on art projects after school. Some clubs like the history club, the Spanish club, and the poetry club are linked to school subjects.

Learning About Clubs

When the school year begins, listen carefully to the morning announcements and check the bulletin board for information about clubs. Your school may have a Club Fair where clubs set up displays in the cafeteria at lunch.

Plan to attend the first meeting to learn what the club is about. Most clubs have flexible membership – you attend meetings when you can. Of course, if you're elected as an officer you'll be expected to attend regularly.

There could be a club that you'd really like to join, but your school doesn't have it. Maybe you're really interested in cartooning or astronomy, but your school doesn't have those clubs. Your school probably has a way for you to start a new club. You would need a teacher to serve as the club sponsor. This is how most clubs get started. Because clubs are based on student interest, they come and go with the styles. One year the chess club will have 25 members, and five years later the club dissolves. Then one student says, "We need to start a chess club," and the club becomes active again. Go to the school office to learn how to start your own interest club.

Service Clubs

Your middle school will probably have clubs that serve the community. These clubs may have car washes or other fundraisers, and then donate the earnings to charity. A service club could pick up trash at the beach, visit the senior center, or help elementary students with their homework. Service clubs give you a chance to help your neighborhood, and have fun, too.

Student Council and Honor Society

Most middle schools have a student council. The student council helps make decisions about the school. Each homeroom will elect a member of the student council. Students in the homeroom will make suggestions to their council member. The student council will discuss all of the suggestions and meet with the principal to talk about them. The student council members report the results back to their homerooms.

Here's an example: you think the school needs more drinking fountains for the students. Usually three or four students are lined-up at the fountain, and sometimes you have to choose between getting a drink of water and being late for class. So, you tell your student council member about this. At the next meeting the student council talks about your suggestion, and even marks a school map with the places the new fountains would go. The student council officers meet with the principal. A few weeks later, there are three new water fountains in the hall – all because you made the suggestion!

As you can see, student council is a big responsibility. Council members have to be good listeners. They also have to be willing to bring ideas before the student council, and report back to the homeroom. If this sounds like something you would enjoy, consider running for a seat on the student council.

Your middle school will probably have an honor society. Students are invited to join the honor society based on their good grades. Some honor societies are very active clubs, with service projects and fun events. Other honor societies meet just once or twice during the year to induct new members. Keep your grades up, and you will probably be invited to join the honor society.

Before we leave this section on clubs, realize that club activities overlap. For example, the photography club is an "interest" club exploring different camera skills. But members might have a service project, providing food for needy families at Thanksgiving. And service clubs also have social events. After cleaning up the beach, the science club could have a great picnic with food and games. It's really up to the club members, the officers, and the sponsor to decide everything a club does during the year.

Sports

Most middle schools have sports teams. Some middle schools have several teams, and other schools have just a few. If you're an athlete, you've probably been a member of several youth-league teams already. But there's nothing quite like wearing a uniform with your school's name on it. You're not just representing your team. You're representing your school.

Tryouts

You will need to try out to earn a place on the team. The coaches will carefully observe your sports skills, and select the best players for the team. If you don't make the team your first year, keep working on your skills. You can try out again next year.

Some middle schools let everyone stay on the team, as long as they attend all of the practices. This is especially true in small schools, where there may just barely be enough athletes to field a team. Larger middle schools have teams just for 6th graders, who compete against 6th graders from other schools. This gives younger students a chance to play and learn more about their sport.

Physical Exam

Before you try out for a sport, you will need to get a physical examination from a doctor. The doctor will examine you, and pronounce you "fit" to join a team. If you know you want to play middle school sports you may want to get your physical over the summer. Contact the school office to get the paperwork. There may be a local doctor who provides free physicals for athletes. This is the doctor's way of supporting sports at the school. The doctor may even come to the school for appointments. When you get your physical, take the paperwork to the coach as soon as possible. And keep a copy for yourself. You may need to turn it in again if you play another sport.

Requirements

There's more to school sports than catching a football or spiking a volleyball. When you wear the team uniform, you will be representing your school. You always want to display good sportsmanship, whether you win or lose. Students who misbehave at a sporting event reflect poorly on the school, and will probably be dismissed from the team.

Student athletes also need to have good grades. This varies from school to school. Typically, you need a "C" or better in all of your classes. Also, students who have discipline or attendance problems are not able to play on sports teams.

Competition

Middle school sports are different from recreational league sports hosted by groups like Little League or YMCA. As stated before, middle school teams have tryouts. Some students make the team, and other students do not. In middle school, there's no requirement for every team member to play in every game. Instead, the coach fields the best team possible at all times. At the end of the recreational league season everyone gets a participation trophy. In middle school trophies are awarded to the league champions and most valuable players.

That's not a knock on recreational league sports. Thousands of boys and girls enjoy playing on rec teams. It's a good place to learn about the game, practice your skills and have lots of fun. Just remember the competitive nature of middle school sports when you decide to try out for a team.

Other Ways to Participate

Even if you're not on a team, you can still be involved with sports at your school. Most teams have positions for student helpers. Teams need scorekeepers, scoreboard operators, and equipment managers. You could even work at the snack stand at the game, or help get the field or court ready for play. Most middle schools have cheerleading squads that cheer at many games.

(Cheerleading is considered a sport at many middle schools, and rightfully so. Modern cheerleading teams feature well-trained, highly-skilled athletes!) So, if you like to be around the game, there are plenty of opportunities in middle school.

Some middle schools have active intramural sports programs. Intramural sports are like clubs that play sports. Here's an example: the PE coach announces that intramural basketball will play on Wednesday afternoons. Each team will have six members. So, you and five of your friends make a team. There are no uniforms or coaches – just you and your friends playing against another group of students from your school. The coach will set the schedule, and probably be the referee. There may be a tournament with a school intramural championship team. It's a lot of fun, and doesn't demand the commitment of playing for the school team.

Your middle school may have "open gym" time one or two nights each week. Open gym could include basketball, volleyball, or weightlifting. A PE coach will be there to supervise. This is a great way to stay physically fit, especially if you don't have PE class during the day.

Activities

Your middle school will probably have more activities in addition to clubs and sports. These activities may require a tryout or application. You will probably need to commit to the activity; in other words, you can't skip a meeting or come and go as you please. The students who join these activities are usually very dedicated, and they enjoy the activities very much.

Music

Middle schools usually have band and chorus programs. Students sing or play their musical instruments during an elective class every day. But there are also rehearsals, performances, and competitions outside the school day. The middle school band may play at the football games and present several concerts throughout the year. The chorus will also have concerts, and will perform for student and community groups. Joining the band or chorus can be a great experience for a middle school student.

Dance Team

Many middle schools have a dance team, where students practice their dance moves and perform at school functions and competitions. The team will probably have tryouts at the beginning of the school year. Dance team membership requires a commitment of time and energy. But, it can be a lot of fun if you like to dance and perform.

Drama Club

Most middle schools have at least one school play each year. Usually, the drama club sponsor (a teacher) will select the play, hold auditions, and supervise rehearsals. The play could be a serious drama, a comedy, or even a musical with singing and dancing. There are many "behind the scenes" jobs for students who really don't want to act on stage.

Publications

Middle schools usually have several publications: yearbook, newspaper, literary magazine, and video crew. Students apply to join the staff, and work on their projects most of the year.

School Dances and Other Events

Your middle school will probably have school dances and other activities during the year. The school may organize a walk-a-thon to raise money for charity. Some schools have canned food drives around the holidays. Your school could have a special science or reading night. You may have the opportunity to display your work in an art show. Even if you're not in the band, the chorus, or the drama club you can still enjoy the concerts and plays. There are many chances to be involved in school activities, even if you're not able to make a long-term commitment.

Activities and Schoolwork

Here's something you should always remember: your schoolwork comes first. If your clubs, activities, or sports teams cause your schoolwork to suffer, then you should cut back on the time you spend on your club/activity/team. That's probably not what you wanted to hear, but it's true. If you have to choose between doing your homework and going to a club meeting, then you need to do your homework.

Commitment

This is very important to think about before joining an activity or sports team that requires a commitment. Ask yourself: will I have time for practice and homework? A club, activity, or sports team is not an excuse for missed assignments.

Choosing Your Activities

You are probably thinking about many clubs, activities, and teams that you'd like to join. Of course, you won't be able to do everything! Here are some tips for choosing your extra-curricular activities.

Ask Questions

Find out all that you can about a club, activity, or sport before joining. Learn how much time it will take. Talk to the sponsor or coach. Try to find out exactly what the club does.

Give It a Try

As we said earlier, most clubs have open membership. You can attend every meeting, or just occasionally. If you think you might enjoy a club, attend a meeting and see for yourself. Tell the sponsor that you're thinking about joining the club. If you enjoy it, great! If not, that's fine too. Clubs are for enjoyment. You will probably find one or two clubs that you really like.

Decide for Yourself

Join the clubs that you want to join. Don't just go along with the crowd. Maybe all of your friends want to join the drama club, but you're more interested in photography. Join the photography club! They will still be your friends. You can take pictures of your friends when they perform in the school play.

You Can't Do Everything!

So, you want to join the band, the chorus, the yearbook staff, student council, the art club, the drama club…. Wow! You get the idea. No one has time to do everything. If you find yourself saying, "Oh no, I have a science club meeting," then it's not fun anymore. Choose the clubs that match your interests, and be willing to take a pass on other opportunities.

Don't Get Discouraged

When it comes to activities and sports, don't get discouraged if things don't work out like you planned. Maybe you really want to be on the student council, but your homeroom elects someone else. Or you've always been the best pitcher on your softball team, but now as a 6th grader you rarely get to play. Or you were the first-chair trumpet player in the elementary band, but now you're the last-chair in the middle school band. Don't get discouraged!

Remember, you were one of the oldest students in elementary school. You are now one of the youngest students in middle school. It's the 8th graders' turn to lead. They were 6th graders once, too. And it won't be too long until it's your turn to quarterback the football team, sing a solo at the chorus concert, or edit the school newspaper. Don't quit just because you're no longer the star. Keep practicing, and you will shine!

Clubs, activities, and sports are great middle school experiences. You can learn more about things you are interested in, work with a team, and represent your school in athletics. Don't miss this great opportunity to enjoy your middle school years.

Your Turn

Are there any middle school clubs that you're interested in joining?

Are you an athlete? If so, what sports are you planning to play in middle school?

What grades do you need to make if you play sports at your middle school?

Below are some clubs and activities that most middle schools have. Place a check beside the activities that you are interested in.

	Band
	Chorus
	Newspaper
	Yearbook
	Dance team
	Drama – school play
	Student council
	Computer club
	Robotics
	Science club
	Reading club
	Art club
	Intramural sports

Conclusion

You're Ready
for Middle School!

Congratulations on completing this book. You've learned a lot of information that will help you be successful in middle school. Let's go over the most important ideas one more time.

In middle school you will have core classes (language arts, math, science, and social studies) and elective classes. Select your elective classes based on your interests. Go to every class ready to learn. Practice your reading skills, your multiplication facts, and your handwriting until you are good at all three. Make plans to study and do your best. Your report card will reflect those efforts. Move responsibly from class to class, and make sure you have your books, folders, and anything else you need. (Chapter 1)

You will have several teachers during the day, with different classrooms, teaching styles, and approaches to technology. Learn what it takes to be successful in every class. Take responsibility for your assignments and always tell the truth. Respect all of the adults who work at your school. (Chapter 2)

Understand that you can be friendly to everyone, but you can't be friends with everyone. You will have acquaintances, friends, and a small group of close friends. Be willing to make new friends, and realize that it takes time to build a friendship. You shouldn't have to conform to someone else's ideas to be their friend. Different interests create changes in friendships in middle school. Avoid exclusive boyfriend-girlfriend relationships, and instead get to know both boys and girls in no-pressure social situations. (Chapter 3)

Middle school teachers and administrators expect students to be able to control themselves, and enjoy the freedom that comes with middle school. Learn the Code of Conduct and the Dress Code for your school. Tell the truth when confronted with mistakes, and apologize to teachers whose classes you have disrupted. Understand the difference between correction and punishment. When faced with punishment, accept it and learn from the situation. (Chapter 4)

Attend school whenever possible. Being an hour tardy to middle school means that you have missed an entire class period. Learn your school's definitions for an excused absence and an unexcused absence. Take responsibility for your make-up work. Remember that the last thirty minutes of the school day are just as important as the first thirty minutes. (Chapter 5)

Your school will provide the opportunity to use technology. Learn the Acceptable Use Policy for your school, and follow the rules. If your school lets you bring your own devices to school, make sure that they do not interrupt your learning. (Chapter 6)

Be proactive when faced with new opportunities and obligations. Do not create stressful situations. Be patient with yourself, and realize that you will eventually adjust. Organizing your books, folders, and book bag can reduce your level of stress. Write important assignments  and meetings in your planner. Remove distractions - like a cell phone or television - when you are doing homework. Don't take unneeded items to school. Listen to the morning announcements and visit the school web site. Use a map to learn your way around campus. (Chapter 7)

Middle schools have many clubs, sports, and activities that you can enjoy. Not everyone makes middle school sports teams. If you don't make the team, practice your skills and try out again next year. Some clubs are casual; you can attend when you want to. Other activities such as band and chorus require a commitment to rehearse and perform. Make sure you know about the commitment level before joining a club. Decide what you want to do based on your interests, and realize that you can't do everything. (Chapter 8)

Welcome to middle school! Get ready for an exciting, rewarding experience. Learn everything, get involved, make friends, and don't forget to have fun.

This is Middle School!

This Is MIDDLE SCHOOL! for Parents

This Is Middle School
for Parents

Welcome to the section written especially for parents of middle school students. Later in this chapter you can find advice related specifically to the topic of each of the previous chapters. But let's begin with some advice on enjoying your child's middle school years.

Be Positive and Encouraging

Moving from the elementary school environment to middle school will be a big change for your son or daughter. Some children adapt to change better than others. You can help your child adjust to their new school by being positive and encouraging. Assure them that they're a great kid, everything will be okay, and they will adjust.

In an attempt to be mature, some upper-elementary students try to solve all of the problems that they face. When the problems are few and the solutions are easy, they can probably manage. But in middle school, things can get a little more involved. Your son or daughter may not have the skill set required to solve certain problems.

So, when a problem presents itself, use the opportunity to support your child and guide them to the appropriate solution. Solve the problem *with* the child, not *for* the child. A parent crusade to the principal's office may be quicker, but working with your child teaches them a valuable skill.

Here's an example: lockers in the middle school locker hall are stacked 3-high – top, middle, and bottom. Of course, the middle lockers are the most desirable. The bottom lockers require squatting, but they're fine, too. But your daughter, who is about 4-foot-6, has inexplicably been assigned a top locker. She's not tall enough to accurately work the combination lock, and using the locker between classes is nearly impossible. She's often late to class, and is missing several homework assignments because she can't get them out of her locker in time. A parent-teacher conference is scheduled to discuss the ongoing tardy problem, the missing assignments, and the falling grades.

This problem seems like an easy fix for the parent: just ask for another locker! But the child's inaction is typical for a 6th grader. This is their locker. Lockers don't change. The parent learns about the locker problem the night before the parent conference. Rather than express outrage that their daughter was given an impossible locker, the parent and child role-play a scene in which the child asks the assistant principal for a new locker.

The next day at school, the girl bravely approaches the assistant principal with her locker dilemma. The assistant principal checks his locker list. Yes, a bottom locker is available right down the hall from your third period class. Will that one be okay?

Another win for the positive, supportive parent – and the daughter, too! Parenting middle school students is a delicate balance. Middle school is the time when boys and girls should learn to think through a situation for themselves, and solve their own problems. As a parent you can help them analyze the issue, evaluate solutions, and role-play different scenarios.

Be a Patient Listener

Part of helping your son or daughter involves patiently listening as they analyze a situation. As a parent who has likely "been there – done that" with the conflict your child is experiencing, it is tempting just to hop right in and reveal the correct answer. Instead, listen to your child and ask probing questions that will guide them to the best solution.

Middle school students are quick to pick up on whether or not the parent is actually involved in the conversation. Make sure that you're not reading the newspaper, watching TV, or checking your Facebook page while your child tells you about his or her day. Ask questions, maintain good eye contact, and repeat back to them what they have told you. If another activity is absolutely necessary, make sure that you and your child are involved in the same task. Many great parent-child conversations have taken place while folding clothes or raking leaves.

Finally, recognize the importance of your child's silent pauses when they are expressing their concerns about a situation. That silence is when their thought processes are likely occurring. Resist the temptation to fill the silence unnecessarily just because the child is not talking. Be a patient listener.

Request Parent-teacher Conferences

Middle school teachers are happy to speak with parents about their children. If you have a question or concern about your child's involvement in school, call the school and ask for a conference with all of your child's teachers. On the surface, this may seem like a drastic step. Really, it's not. Teachers would much rather address situations before they become too serious. Thirty minutes spent with your child's teachers can solve many issues, and open lines for future communication.

Keep Teachers Informed

Inform your child's teachers about life-changing situations your child is facing. Examples would include death or illness of a family member, changes in the family structure, or a history of medical problems your child has faced. Don't assume that your teacher is aware of these issues. You can trust the teachers to maintain confidentiality in personal situations. (If you have concerns about this, make sure the teachers and administrators understand your desire for privacy.) Teachers can be great allies in observing and reporting to you how your child is functioning daily at school.

Be a School Supporter

Your middle school places great value on the support you give them in your home, at work, and in the community. Schools spend a great deal of time, money, and energy communicating with parents and creating a learning environment that supports the community's values and goals. However, in any man-made system there will be a few bumps in the road. If you are experiencing a negative situation with the school, please schedule a conference with the administration as soon as possible. Don't assume that "they just don't care."

Think about the locker situation described earlier in this chapter. As you read it, you may have asked yourself why anyone in their right mind gave that little girl a top locker! That's a valid question. Understand that over 500 lockers were assigned on orientation day. Even if 10 students were assigned lockers that didn't fit their needs, 98% of the time a correct locker was assigned. More important than the initial goof was the school's willingness to quickly solve the problem once they were made aware of it.

(And by the way, the locker example is a true story. The girl was not able to attend orientation day, and her rather tall friend obtained a locker for her.)

Rumors have a way of becoming more sensational with every repetition. If something doesn't make sense to you, ask the school administration for clarification. The principal will be more than happy to correct any misunderstandings and work toward a fair solution to any problems your child is experiencing.

Volunteer (if possible)

There are many opportunities for parents to volunteer at middle school. In fact, most middle schools would find it extremely difficult to function without a group of dedicated volunteers.

Most middle schools have a volunteer coordinator – an administrator or faculty member who serves as the contact person for volunteers and matches them with opportunities requested by teachers. The school will probably require some type of affidavit or background check. Don't be dismayed – that's just the world we live in.

Listing all of the middle school volunteer opportunities would be nearly impossible. Every school is different. In addition to the traditional long-term opportunities (room parent, PTA officer, reading tutor, etc.) you will probably find short-term or one-day volunteer requests at middle school. Here are some examples:

- Assisting in distribution and collection of band and chorus uniforms
- Working the concession stand at a basketball game
- Supervising students on the playground at the annual walk-a-thon
- Helping new students find their classes on the first day of school
- Serving as a guest speaker on career day
- Escorting a class on a field trip
- Building sets and scenery for the school play.

Contact the school volunteer coordinator and tell them your interests. They can probably find a way to use your talents and abilities.

The remainder of this chapter contains information for parents related specifically to the topic of each of the previous chapters.

Chapter 1: Your Middle School Classes

A schedule with six different classes in six different rooms with six different teachers is one of the most exciting characteristics of the transition to middle school. It also has the potential to produce anxiety in your son or daughter. As a parent, you can certainly help make the move to middle school a pleasant change.

Your child may come home the first day of school saying things like:

> "I don't know anybody in any of my classes."
> "I don't like any of my teachers."
> "I got lost 3 times today."
> "There's no way I can get to class on time."
> "I'll never be able to remember this schedule."
> ...and more.

Your first instinct as a parent may be to list the grievances and make an appointment with the principal to get all of these problems solved. Your child needs to be in classes with his/her friends, with teachers they already know and like, in classrooms right next door to one another. They need 3 classes, not 6, and at least 10 minutes between classes...

Can you imagine 200 parents lined-up outside the principal's office with these demands on the second day of school?

Realistically, your child probably isn't looking for you to solve their "problems." Your child wants to hear that everything will be okay. They are totally out of their comfort zone, thrown from the cocoon of elementary school into the middle school jungle. (That's how they see it, anyway!) Your job as a parent is to listen, and provide assurances that everything will be fine.

"I don't know anybody in any of my classes." You've always been great at making friends. I'm sure you will find new friends in your classes. You can't be friends with everyone, but tomorrow try to make a friend in every class. Just say "hi" and ask their name. You're a great kid, and anyone in the class would be fortunate to have you for a friend.

"I don't like any of my teachers." You probably just need to get to know them. In elementary school, you had only one new teacher every year. This year you have six! Give them a chance. And please let me know if you feel uncomfortable in the class. I'm here to help.

"I got lost 3 times today." Oh, I'm sorry – but you must have found your way, because here you are! I remember I got lost my first day of middle school. But by the end of the week, I could find my way all around campus. I'm sure you'll be able to do that too. Remember, if you get lost find a teacher – any teacher. I'm sure they'll be happy to help.

"There's no way I can get to class on time." I think you probably can. You just need to get used to your schedule. Do you have a map of the school? Let's look at it, and make sure you're taking the best routes. Let's figure out when you really need to go to your locker. We can solve this puzzle.

"I'll never be able to remember this schedule." Sure you will! You're smart, and you've done harder things before. Remember when you memorized the 50 states and capitals? Let's look at your schedule – I'll help you.

Should you ignore your child's legitimate concerns? Of course not! If your child is still lost, friendless, tardy, or convinced that they'll never like their teachers after the first week of school, then certainly you want to set-up a conference with the principal, the counselor, and the teachers. You know your child. Never ignore a threat, or put them in a dangerous situation.

Just realize that 99% of student concerns and anxieties are resolved during the first week of school. As a parent, you can provide the loving, supportive home environment that encourages adjustment to this new situation.

Pretty soon, you'll be hearing, "Mom, I didn't get lost at all today! Can my new friend spend the night this weekend?"

Chapter 2: Teachers, Administrators, and Other Adults

Becoming accustomed to the teaching styles of six new teachers can be a challenging experience for middle schoolers. And it's quite possible that your son or daughter will come home one day saying that they don't like one of their teachers or classes.

As a parent, it is important for you to determine why your child isn't enjoying certain classes. The reflex action might be to go to the school and demand a schedule change. Realize that most 11 or 12 year olds are capable of experiencing complex emotions, but not very good at describing or expressing those emotions. You can probably learn a lot by asking your child thoughtful questions and listening carefully to the answers.

Sometimes parents begin with "Why don't you like this class?" Unfortunately, that doesn't always get the needed answers. Instead, try "What's happening in the class that you don't like?" or "When do you feel uncomfortable?" Ask your son or daughter to describe what happens right before they begin to feel uncomfortable in the class. This will help you understand your child's frame of mind, and the reasons behind their dissatisfaction.

It is important to realize the differences in elementary school and middle school when listening to your child talk about his or her teachers and classes. Elementary teachers take on a more parental role than do middle school and high school teachers. In elementary school, students may become very emotionally close to their teachers. Elementary teachers often give a "hug or high-five" to all of their students every day. That is very unlikely to happen in middle school. Do middle school teachers care about your child? Absolutely! However, middle school classes focus more on the class content and less on building relationships. If your child says, "My teacher hates me," but really can't name a specific reason, it's probably because they aren't making the emotional ties to the teacher that they did in elementary school.

Realize also that students have different definitions for some common words. The most obvious example is "yell." Twenty years ago, the word yell meant raising the voice level in a forceful way. However, now students will use the word "yell" to describe someone being corrected in a firm manner. A student might say, "My teacher yelled at me after class," when in fact the teacher asked the student to stay after class and calmly and firmly asked them to improve their behavior. Another word that some students use is "mean." A student might describe a teacher as "mean," when in fact the teacher believes that the rules of the classroom should be followed, or the teacher gives homework every night. Twenty years ago, the word "mean" was used to describe someone who had malevolent intentions, and treated people cruelly.

So, imagine your child comes home and says, "I hate my science class. The teacher is so mean. He yelled at me today." Your first reaction might be to hop in the car, drive to the school, and pick a fight with the first person you see! However, a few thoughtful questions might reveal that your child is having trouble with the science lessons, doesn't understand the homework, and was corrected for misbehaving in class.

As always, you know your own child. Don't ignore obvious warning signs of problems in school. Just remember that your child is facing the challenge of adapting to several different teaching styles in an unfamiliar setting.

Many parents find it beneficial to role-play student-adult conversations with their child. Some students have a great deal of experience talking with adults, and others don't. Students lacking this experience may not advocate for themselves in important situations. Other students may offend the adult with an unintentionally disrespectful approach. Create a set of scenarios, and ask your child to role-play the student or the adult. This strategy lets you model the correct behavior and gives your child the opportunity to practice in a pressure-free environment.

Chapter 3: Your Friends

As a parent of a middle schooler, it is important for you to know your child's friends. The challenge is to accomplish this task while giving your child space to make friends on their own.

The easiest way to get to know your child's friends is to invite them into your home. Arrange a pizza party at your house. Your son or daughter can invite several of their friends for an afternoon of food and fun. Observe their interactions while you serve pizza and refill soda glasses. Learn the names of the boys and girls, and invite their parents into your home when they pick-up their children. This is especially important if your son or daughter has replaced his/her friends with a new group.

Be aware of any age discrepancies between your child and their friends. Socially, there's a big difference between a sixth grader and a ninth grader. Also, be watchful of friends with destructive habits, or those who seem to have no accountability to adults.

Watch and listen for overly-emotional or dramatic friend relationships. If your son or daughter is troubled or upset after talking to their friend, it may be the sign of an unhealthy friendship. Talk to your son or daughter. They may be carrying the burden of their friend's problems.

Finally, help your child set boundaries for their friendships. In middle school, boys and girls experiment with clothing styles, haircuts, music, and hobbies. Make sure that your child isn't succumbing to pressure from friends to dress a certain way or to change their tastes to please others. You can certainly help your child develop healthy perspectives and attitudes about friendship.

Chapter 4: Behavior in Middle School

Schools write and publish a Code of Conduct. This code outlines expected behavior, and consequences of misbehavior. The Code of Conduct is in place to insure that the school functions in a safe, orderly manner.

Students typically receive a copy of the Code of Conduct during the first week of school. Many schools publish the code on the school web site. As a parent, you should obtain a copy of the Code of Conduct and become very familiar with the school rules and the consequences for breaking these rules. Your child will be held accountable to the standards and consequences outlined in the code. If you have any questions or concerns you should express them immediately to the school administration. Don't wait until confronted with an unfortunate situation to voice your challenges to the code.

Discipline issues at elementary school and middle school are handled somewhat differently. Elementary discipline gives a fair amount of consideration to immaturity and impulse control, and rightly so. However, by the time a child enters middle school, they are expected to have a certain control over their impulses, and act appropriately for their age. Simply put, in middle school there is less tolerance for immature behavior. An immature middle school student may be confused when silly behavior is considered inappropriate. Very few middle school teachers would enjoy behaviors such as hopping around the classroom, making funny animal noises, or burping loudly in the classroom.

Along the same line, misbehaviors such as stealing and willful disobedience may be considered much more serious in middle school. When an elementary student steals a classmate's pencil box, they have to give it back and say, "I'm sorry." Middle school students will probably face a more serious penalty. An elementary student who refuses to come in from recess will likely lose his recess time for a week. A middle school student defying a teacher in a similar way would likely face suspension. You can help your son or daughter understand these differences.

Does that mean that middle school administrators prowl the hallways, just waiting to pounce on the little sixth graders? Of course not! Middle school administrators enjoy providing the guidance that students need to be successful. A teacher or administrator who doesn't like children usually has a very short career in education. However, middle school teachers and administrators realize that in a few short years the children in front of them will be in high school, and in the "real world" shortly thereafter. No one is served when the middle school allows behavior that will be unacceptable in the child's future.

An important topic was mentioned briefly near the end of the chapter, but it's very important for parents. Simply stated: allow the school to appropriately punish your child for violations of school rules. That's a difficult sentence to read (and to write, too) but it is very important. If your child makes a mistake at school (such as simple classroom disruption) you might be very tempted to try to arrange for a dismissal of the punishment. This effort is typically counter-productive. It undermines the authority of the school, and increases the likelihood that the child will break the rules again. When teachers and staff members report a violation of the Code of Conduct, they expect the consequences outlined in the code to be administered. The school has an obligation to implement the Code of Conduct fairly to every student.

The flip-side of the same coin reveals the concept of double-punishment. In your well-placed desire for improving your child's conduct at school, carefully consider any additional punishment that you administer at home. In the student section of Chapter 4, a scenario was presented in which a student throws a paper airplane in class, and receives a 30-minute detention for class disruption. Should you implement additional punishment at home? Of course that is up to you, the parent. However, realize that it is possible to over-punish minor misbehaviors. An after-school detention can be quite unpleasant. The student typically sits in a supervised detention room, and must be quiet for the entire time. They can read or do homework, but they cannot talk. While in detention, a student is missing free time with their friends. Some students miss team practices or club meetings while in detention. A student who hasn't been in trouble before is typically very embarrassed to be in the detention room. For most students, one detention is enough to convince them to change their ways.

As a parent, you know your child. Additional punishment at home may be productive, or counter-productive. The key is to get the child's attention and correct the behavior without inducing a feeling of hopelessness.

To repeat a sentence stated several times in the student chapter: most middle school students never get in trouble at school. Knowledge of the school's Code of Conduct will help your child understand the school rules, and the consequences of rule violations.

Chapter 5: Attendance

Regular attendance is very important in middle school. Encourage your child to attend school every day possible. Missing a day of middle school means that your child is missing several classes, each with activities, assignments, and evaluations.

As a parent, you can have a great influence on your child's attendance. Some parents keep their elementary children out of school for shopping trips or recreational activities. This practice, although well intentioned, would probably be detrimental to your child's middle school education.

Along the same line, some elementary parents check their children out in the middle of the day for a long lunch or check them out early to avoid the traffic. These practices will also remove your child from important educational opportunities.

When it comes to tardies, appointments and family trips, most middle school students have very little control over their absences. Read this chapter in the student portion of this book, and make every effort to have your child in class as often as possible.

Certainly, some absences are unavoidable due to illness. Others, such as important family and religious functions, are important to the child's social development. Most students can easily make-up work missed due to these occasional absences.

Chapter 6: Using Technology

Buying Technology

Your child will probably use technology every day in middle school. Realize that you don't need to buy computers, tablets, and smartphones for your child to use at school. Whenever a child needs to use technology, the school will provide those devices. However, if you decide to buy a computer or a tablet for your child, there are probably several teachers at the school qualified to help you make the best choice.

Student Cell Phones

You may decide to provide a cell phone for your child to take to school. Consider the type of phone and phone service that you give your child. You can certainly talk and text with your child using a smartphone. Realize that the smartphone can also be used by your child to play games, watch movies, and use social media at school. A clever middle school student quickly learns how to download the Netflix app onto the smartphone and access the family account. If the child has a generous data plan, he or she can spend all day on the Internet and miss a lot of instruction.

As an adult, you probably have the ability to watch movies, play games, and check Facebook all day on your smartphone. But you don't, because you are mature, and you fight that temptation. You realize that your work productivity would suffer, and your boss would certainly disapprove. Unfortunately, most middle school students lack that maturity. Most teachers can tell a story about an otherwise responsible student who got in trouble with a smartphone and a data plan.

So, what's the solution? You may consider a simple talk-and-text cell phone for your child. These phones are $20 or less, and prepaid service plans are also inexpensive. And if the phone is lost or broken, a replacement costs only a few dollars. Your child will still be able to talk on the phone and send and receive texts. That's probably why you want them to have a cell phone in the first place – so that they can contact *you*. A simple talk-and-text phone removes the temptation to play games and watch videos while at school.

Following the Technology Rules

Take a few minutes to understand the school's technology rules, and talk about them with your child. Determine if students are allowed to have cell phones at school. If so, where and when can they use them?

Also, make sure your communications with your child allow them to follow the school rules. Realize that if you send your child a text message during the school day, they may not be able to see it or answer it for an hour or more. Most teachers have witnessed middle school students sneaking a text in class. More often than not, they are answering a parent's text. That puts teachers in a very awkward situation: the student has violated a school rule while being attentive to a parent's request. Of course, the school office would gladly relay a message from parent to child. Texting is easier and faster, but may be against the rules.

Social Media

During the middle school years, many students become interested in social media – most notably Facebook. As a parent, you may or may not be familiar with Facebook yourself. Be ready to provide advice and guidance to your child on the use of social media. Help them understand what is appropriate on Facebook, and what is not. Most importantly, make sure that their social media experiences are responsible and safe.

Chapter 7: Getting Organized and Staying Informed

Getting Organized

Organization is a big part of the transition from elementary school to middle school. The elementary take-home folders that held papers, teacher notes, and permission slips aren't used in middle school. There are no more classroom newsletters to inform parents about upcoming assignments and activities. Instead of a cubby and a desk, your child will have a book bag and a locker. A jacket left at elementary school is probably in the classroom. A jacket left at middle school could be anywhere. In order to function in middle school, a student needs to be organized and informed.

Almost all middle schools use spiral-bound planners to help students' organization skills. In some schools, the planner is an informal tool for students to use as they wish. Other schools require students to write their assignments in their planners each week. As a parent, you can follow-up by checking your son or daughter's planner, and asking to see completed assignments.

Be sensitive to your child's level of stress. If they find middle school stressful, poor organization skills may be to blame. Question your child to determine the source of the stress. The daily pace of middle school is challenging for some students. Read the student chapter, and be ready to offer your advice.

You can help your child get organized at home by providing a specific place for their school materials and a distraction-free homework environment. Students who take an hour or more to complete a brief homework assignment are often trying to solve math problems while watching TV and answering text messages. As a parent, you can help limit these distractions.

Help your child resist the urge to overload their book bag with unnecessary school supplies and personal items. The first step is distinguishing between need levels: *I need this*, *I might need this*, and *I could possibly need this sometime in the future*. Some students have active imaginations, and will stuff their book bags with the solution to every brainstormed problem. Insist on a weekly book bag "dump out" with extra items staying at home and garbage going in the trashcan.

Finally, remember this is a growth process for your child. Even the best elementary students will need to learn middle school organization skills. Offer advice and suggestions, and don't hesitate to become more involved if your child is still struggling with organization skills after the first month of school.

Staying Informed

As a parent, it's important for you to stay informed as well. The planner and the school web site are valuable tools in this effort. You can check the school's web site each week for updates on clubs, sports, and other school events. Most middle schools have a number of activities open to incoming middle school students. The web site will likely feature the e-mail addresses of your child's teachers.

Most schools have computer-based grade books. Student grades are available for online viewing. It would be a good idea to check your child's grades on a regular basis. Most parents would like notification if their child's grades were slipping. In middle school, the online grade book is that notification. Elementary teachers have 20 or 25 students, and often talk with parents on a weekly basis. A middle school teacher with 125 students can't keep that pace. Checking grades online is a quick way to determine your child's progress. You can also check for missing assignments.

Chapter 8: Clubs, Sports, and Activities

Clubs, sports, and activities can be among the most enjoyable facets of a middle schooler's week. Many students find their niche when they join the band, play on a sports team, or discover a club that matches their interest. Students who are otherwise not very interested in school become motivated by extra-curricular opportunities. And frequently, student athletes "hit the books" to maintain their eligibility. Clubs, sports, and activities are typically very positive experiences for middle school students.

As a parent, it's up to you to help your child strike a balance between schoolwork and extracurricular activities. Time is the commodity involved. You can teach your child to make wise use of their available time. Reinforce the concept mentioned in the student chapter: schoolwork comes first. Many parents have to make the difficult decision to curtail or eliminate their child's after-school commitments until a balance is found.

Be aware of indicators that your child might be spending too much time on extracurricular activities. Those symptoms would include:

- falling grades
- missing homework assignments
- stress-filled reactions when you ask the child about the activity
- scheduling conflicts between activities.

Middle school students need to learn that they can't do everything. In elementary school it is possible to participate in all or most school activities because there are fewer opportunities, fewer practices, and less homework. Middle school isn't that way. Talk with your child about all of the extracurricular activities that interest them, and encourage them to select one or two activities. They can always increase their involvement if they find that they don't have enough to do.

As students move from elementary school to middle school, understand that they will be in extracurricular activities with students two or three years older, and perhaps more physically developed than incoming sixth graders. This is especially relevant in sports. Simply stated, the all-star elementary athlete might not make the middle school team. The captain of the Little League cheerleading squad might not be selected as a middle school cheerleader. Why aren't these students selected? Because they are competing with older, more experienced students. There are likely dozens of students in 7th or 8th grade who are better athletes than the student who was in elementary school just a few weeks ago.

Unfortunately, some students become discouraged and give up on their dreams at the first sign of failure. As a parent, it is important for you to help you child understand why they have moved from "king or queen of elementary school" to a less-prestigious status. Encourage them to keep practicing and to develop the skills that will make them successful in middle school. Also, you can help your child investigate opportunities for 6th grade school teams and community-based athletic leagues.

Of course, if you have a question about team selection or extracurricular opportunities, schedule an appointment with the school principal. Most sports team rosters are created after a rigorous, score-based tryout. Unlike recreational leagues, in school athletics not everyone makes the team every year. Most teams are limited to a certain number of members. To include your child would probably mean excluding a more-deserving boy or girl. The process is a learning opportunity.

Finally, remember that at the middle school level most club sponsors and coaches are performing this duty for little or no additional pay. They coach or sponsor an extracurricular activity because they enjoy working with middle school students, and they believe that an involved student is a successful student.

About the Author

Keith Kyker (M.Ed.) is an experienced classroom teacher and library media specialist. After a successful 30-year teaching career in Florida, Keith moved to Alaska where he taught for two years. He now lives and teaches in Tennessee.

He is an experienced conference speaker and workshop presenter. He has presented over 200 sessions at educational conferences in 14 states. He served on committees that designed the National Board for Professional Teaching Standards (NBPTS) evaluations for library media specialists, and the Florida Teacher Certification Exam. He is a former Okaloosa County (Florida) School District Teacher of the Year.

Keith is the author of several educational technology textbooks published by Libraries Unlimited, including *Teaching Digital Photography* (2014.) In 2014 he founded the publishing company Third Stream Press. *This is Middle School* is the third book published by this company.

For information about inviting Keith to speak at your conference, workshop, or school, send e-mail to keithkyker@yahoo.com.

Acknowledgments

The author would like to thank the following educators for their advice during the creation of this book.

Denise Beachem
Caroline Carpenter
Jill Dickey
Cheryl Duty
Erin B. Evans
Kathy Harper
Stacey Lavin
Gianna Giusti McCune
Dennis Samac
Libby Swain
Carol Szklarski
Pat Thomas
Molly Thompson

Ordering Information
Discount Price

A discount is available for orders of 50 or more books from a single customer. To receive this discount, books must be purchased directly from the publisher.

For information about this discount, please send e-mail to keithkyker@yahoo.com.

Discount subject to discontinuation without notice.

Photo/illustration credits

<u>Illustrations</u>

All cartoon illustrations licensed by Dollar Photo Club, copyright Denis_PC.

<u>Photographs</u>

All photographs licensed by Dollar Photo Club, copyright the following:

Page 20: Rob / Page 22: Tyler Olson / Page 29: BillionPhotos.com / Page 32: Cheryl Casey / Page 35: Antonio Diaz / Page 41: Michael Jung / Page 44: Tiero / Page 45: Thomas Perkins, Igor / Page 47: Monkey Business / Page 49: Rob / Page 50: AlJohn784 / Page 51: Monkey Business, Wavebreak Media Micro / Page 52: Sepy / Page 53: Shot Studio, Wavebreak Media Micro / Page 58: DURIS Guillaume / Page 61: Monkey Business / Page 63: Thomas Perkins / Page 68: Monkey Business / Page 72: Marzanna Syncerz / Page 76: Rob / Page 77: Kevin Mayer / Page 80: Monkey Business / Page 83: Sabe Photo / Page 85: Lexxxx37 / Page 86: Winai Tepsuttinum / Page 87: Sabe Photo / Page 88: Hugo Felix / Page 89: Antonio Diaz / Page 90: Auremar, Syda Productions / Page 95: Africa Studio / Page 96: Gorilla / Page 99: Michael Jung / Page 106: Tyler Olson / Page 107: Tolgatezcan / Page 108: Thomas Perkins / Page 110: Yanlev / Page 112: Sryantoslav Lypynskyy / Page 114: Wavebreak Media Micro / Page 118: Cristovao31 / Page 120: Antonio Diaz / Page 121: Karen Roach / Page 122: Firma V / Page 123: Ivonne Wierink / Page 124: Szasz Fabian Jozsef / Page 125: Thomas Perkins / Page 126: Monkey Business / Page 127: Eleonore H / Page 129: Olegkruglyak3 / Page 130: Syda Productions / Page 134: Tyler Olson / Page 135: Monkey Business, Garry0305 / Page 136: Mangostock, Rob / Page 137: Lisa F. Young / Page 138: Monkey Business / Page 139: Monkey Business / Page 140: View Apart / Page 141: Highway Starz / Page 142: Monkey Business / Page 144: Karelnoppe / Page 145: Pixelhead Photo / Page 149: Lisa F. Young / Page 150: Antonio Diaz / Page 151: Vitalina Rybakova, Alice Rawson.

Made in the USA
Lexington, KY
03 August 2018